To Liz

Many thanks fo
years at Mt. ???? and
????. You served both churches
well, and now you have moved
on. Your prayers are with you
and we just want to say
Thank you. Every blessing.
BMAB
25/4/23

DISCIPLINE:
THE KEY TO ONE MAN'S TRANSFORMATION

DISCIPLINE:

THE KEY TO ONE MAN'S TRANSFORMATION

MELVIN A. BROOKS

Discipline: The Key to One Man's Transformation
By Melvin A. Brooks

Cover Design by Adam Charles Brooks (campsite.bio / adambrux)

© Copyright 2019
SAINT PAUL PRESS, DALLAS, TEXAS
www.stpaulpresspublishers.com

First Printing, 2019.

Unless otherwise indicated, all scripture quotations are taken from the Holy Bible King James Version (KJV). Public domain.

ISBN: 9798655196575

Printed in the U.S.A.

DEDICATION

Ms. Eliza Smith

With love and admiration, I dedicate this book

to my loving grandmother, Ms. Eliza Smith,

affectionately called "Ms. Liza" or "Sis".

The facts of life define her as my grandmother, but to me,

she was 'My Mama,' the woman that raised me single-handedly.

Adamant that she would keep me

while my parents travelled from Jamaica to England.

My Mama reared me until I turned 16,

and she is the reason I am the man I am today.

Mama taught me life's principles of care, forgiveness, hard work, purpose,

respect, education, and most importantly, faith, love and prayer.

Mama told me I was a disciplined boy, and I believed her.

ACKNOWLEDGEMENTS

Writing this book has been an arduous task, and it would not have materialised without the input and support of those around me.

First and foremost, I give all honor and praise to the Almighty God, the Lord Jesus Christ. I thank God, the source of my strength, my provider, father, and friend who has never left my side. Without the Lord on my side, I would not have been blessed with the opportunities bestowed upon my life. I am so grateful the Lord allowed my path to cross with so many wonderful people. It is because of his grace and mercy that I can share this book with you.

I am so grateful for the love and support of my beautiful wife of 42 years, Yvonne Elizabeth Brooks. This book would not have been possible without your prayers and encouragement. To my children, Rebecca Linton, Adam Brooks, and Matthew Brooks, you have been so loyal and have always believed in me. I am honored to be your father. Adam, thank you for designing the perfect cover for my book; your work never disappoints.

I am eternally grateful for my parents Joshua Emmanuel and Catherine Rebecca Brooks for bringing me into this world and loving me. The support of my siblings has also been valuable, thank you.

To my story editor, under the alias of Ruth-Ann James-Eldrick, thank you for persevering with me and sacrificing your time to make this happen. You have been committed week in and week out. Ddruooe Renders, as the second editor, your time and expertise are highly appreciated. To Britanie Boyd, thank you for making yourself available in the early stages of this process and thank you to Celestine Francis for all of your work.

A huge thank you to my former headteachers in Jamaica, Mr. Scott, and Mrs. Merlyn V Douglas. Every lesson learned served a great purpose in molding me into the man I am today.

To my New J family, my Jabula family and all those who have prayed and encouraged me over the years, thank you.

To every reader with this book in hand, it is my sincere prayer that the lessons shared will

Transform Your Life. Forever.

FOREWORD

Most of the time, when I meet someone for the first time, I feel like I've already met them. I don't mean this literally but metaphorically. It's like I've met their type before, either in character, attitude, or actions. However, this was not the case when meeting Bishop Melvin Brooks. There's something so special about him that distinguishes him from anyone else I know or anyone that I've ever met. I am not referring to his title, his physical appearance, or his accomplishments though they are many. Instead, I found a rarity in his persona, which reflects a combination of self-discipline, personal drive, and an authentic desire for others' success. Somehow this three-punch combo uniquely shows up and reverberates through every area of his life.

Where most people approach their lives by acting out of their various roles, i.e., pastor role, husband or father role Bishop Brooks doesn't. Instead of conforming to any one role, he conforms his multiple roles to who he is as a man, and he does it intentionally. For instance, as you will discover in this book, Bishop Brooks finds delights in putting God first, his wife second, children third, and church after. Where many preachers are tempted to put their "ministry role" to a church first, Bishop Brooks demonstrates he is a minister, both at church and home, by how he serves God, his wife, family, and local assembly. Bishop Brooks gives us an example of an ordered, intergraded, and well-disciplined life that embodies a biblical paradigm of priorities. In doing this, he's creating a lasting legacy that transcends any one life area alone.

Most people think legacy is about worldly things when, in reality, legacy is all about people. My friend Dr. Samuel R. Chand says, "legacy isn't about the what, it's about the who." Bishop Brooks exemplifies this principle as he lives out his Mama's legacy. Mama deposited Christian principles into Melvin her grandson, modeled savvy industrious business practices and a strong work ethic. Although Mama is gone to be with the Lord, in a way, her presence remains alive, as seen in Bishop Brooks' work ethic and God-honoring life. Bishop Brooks is moving Mama's legacy forward all the while creating his own.

The foundation of his discipline, demeanor, and devotion instilled as a young boy in Jamaica has produced a steady, even-tempered man that provokes all those he touches to become their best selves. Anyone who knows Bishop Brooks knows he will call you out, in a way that only he can; one that makes you aim higher and strive to be more. In the same way, he calls people out; he also generously pours into them. His steady deposits into his family, the local church, aged women, inmates, and pastors around the world, including yours truly, confirms that Melvin Alphonso Brooks is building his legacy now through how he believes in and loves people. It is this service to others that demonstrates, as he emphatically declares in this work, that he doesn't merely exist, but he's actually living! Even still, his life hasn't been without its share of hardships.

Bishop Brooks transparently shares his trials from boyhood when he internalized misconceptions of being born left-handed to manhood when he was diagnosed with cancer. However, he shows the reader, through a disciplined lifestyle, your trials come to transform or refine you and don't have to define you or your future. Instead, Bishop Brooks gives us a model of a self-controlled life that perseveres through pain, breaks past limiting beliefs, triumphs through life's hardest trials and comes out better for them.

In our book, *Weathering the Storm: Leading in Uncertain Times*, Dr. Samuel R. Chand and I teach change is inevitable, but growth is optional. You see, everybody goes through storms, but not everybody grows through them. Similarly, *Discipline: The Key to One Man's Transformation* reminds us every day we have a choice to make. Will we haphazardly breeze through our lives or discipline ourselves daily so that we become all we were created to be?

I've noticed your life doesn't change in a day but daily. It's not our big moments that make or break us; it's the little things we do or don't do, over-time, consistently. Someone once said, "life is 10% what happens to you and 90 percent what happens in you". Perhaps, our commitment to being disciplined is what defines the 90 percent of what happens within us and consequently, what ultimately defines our entire lives.

Regardless of what has defined your life so far, Bishop Brooks shows us it's not too late. Through discipline and intentionality, you can still live into the person you could have been all along. In fact, if you're hungry for divine purpose, craving a life of meaning, and desire to fully live in ways that matter, I've got good news for you! Right now, in your hands, you're holding the answer to your prayers and a road-map for your journey.

My prayer for all those who read *Discipline: The Key to One Man's Transformation* is that you too will experience change. I hope that every reader does what Mama instructed Bishop Brooks to do, and he's done with this seminal work, "take what you know and teach someone else." As we all do, may we see young men, students, husbands, pastors, families, churches, and even communities transformed. For who knows just how wide the impact of this great work will resound. Perhaps one day, I'll meet someone for the first time and have the joy of saying, "I've met you before in the person of Melvin Alphonso Brooks, for discipline transformed your life forever too."

Dr. Don Brawley III

Canaan Land Church Int'l, Lead Pastor

Influencers Global, LLC- President

CONTENTS

∞ THE MAN ∞

∞ THE MESSAGE ∞

∞ THE MINISTRY ∞

CHAPTER I

HE WAS A DISCIPLINED BOY

Parents that discipline their children lay the foundation for responsible adulthood. Discipline is not only good for children, but it is necessary for their happiness and well-being. Without discipline, children lack the tools required to navigate relationships and challenges in life, such as self-discipline, respect for others, and the ability to respect authority. When discipline is not developed during the early childhood stage of life, the child lacks the required skills to face challenges and improve relationships. Parents that introduce discipline in the early stages of childhood set the groundwork for their child's happiness and joy. It has been reported that children that are not disciplined are often unhappy, angry, and have a hard time getting along with others.

The key to discipline is LOVE. Therefore, I believe that love and discipline go hand-in-hand. The following traits and abilities are evident in the lives of children who have been given a firm, yet loving guidance:

- A disciplined child has more self-control and self-sufficiency.
- A disciplined child is more responsible and enjoys "being good" and helping others at home, at school and in the world at large.
- A disciplined child is more self-confident. They know their opinions and feelings will be heard, and that their parents love them even when they make mistakes.
- A disciplined child knows they are held accountable for their mistakes or misbehavior and are more likely to make good choices because they want to, not because they fear punishment. disciplined child is pleasant to be around, and they are more

likely to have an easier time making acquaintances.

By the age of 3, my Grandmother's labour of love had begun to mould discipline in my life. Back in Jamaica, she and I were walking up "Long Hill," and after making it to the top of the hill, a lady came along and offered me a piece of fruit. To the stranger's surprise, I did not take the fruit from her, and she could not believe it. My Grandmother explained to her that I am a disciplined boy and that a no from me, meant just that, NO. From then on my Grandmother's words, *'he is a disciplined boy,'* were etched into my soul. I started to believe it, and because my Grandmother said it, I, in turn, felt it. I realised my grandmother was disciplined, and my behaviour was simply following her footsteps, so I started behaving that way.

The Power of Influence

The power of influence is a primary ingredient that is often overlooked when we consider the entire makeup of who we are and what moulds and shapes us as individuals. The people we interact with, the places we attend, and the experiences we encounter can either provide a positive or a negative influence that impacts the rest of our lives. The impact gained directly affects what flows out of us, inevitably changing the lives of others around us.

Unfortunately, there was a period in my life where negative influences led me to believe that I was doomed for hell. While growing up in Jamaica, I was told that because I was left handed, I was going to hell. Over and again, I was reminded that because the Bible declares that the goats were on the left and the sheep were on the right; my left hand had me doomed for hell. The negative influences continued to speak ill over my life. I was often criticised for having fair skin, knotty hair, and a stuttering impediment. I was told I would never get married and never have a family. The more negative I heard in my life, the more I believed it. I believed it to the point of contemplating actions to justify going to hell since I did not assign myself to hell. As far as I knew, I didn't ask to be born, and I certainly didn't ask to be left-handed. Originally I planned to do something I felt was worthwhile going to hell for. I pondered my actions, and one day, I sat on a wall, and before I could make any ridiculous error, the thought came to me, "But God is greater than man." At that time in my life, I had no idea what that meant, but the thought was enough to get me off of the wall. I walked away and changed my thoughts of doing evil. I didn't know it then, but the Lord spoke Job 33:12 into my spirit; *"Behold, in this thou art not just: I will answer thee, that God is greater than man."* The enemy had planted words of evil around me to make me believe I would fail, but the Lord spoke to me to remind me that He would always be the number one man in my life.

As I look back over my life, I can identify the individuals that I consider as powerful influencers in my life: my grandmother, Ms. Eliza Smith, her pastor from the Baptist Church, Pastor Henry, my first head teacher, Mr. Scott, and my second and last head teacher, Mrs. M. V. Douglas. These four people were influential in moulding and shaping me into the man that I am today.

The Four Influential Figures Of My Life

I. My Grandmother

The age of three is the earliest that I can recall that I, Melvin Alphonso Brooks, existed. From what my parents told me, I only survived childhood by God's grace. An early illness threatened my life as an infant, but God kept me here. Greatness must have been in God's plan for my life because somebody tried to kill me by using witchcraft when I was a baby. The enemy had a plan to destroy me, but the power of prayer kept me alive. I was prayed for, and the enemy was uncovered, they were able to name the person who attempted to take my life. I'm so grateful for an earthly father that has a relationship with Jesus Christ. My father, Bishop Dr. Joshua Emmanuel Brooks, petitioned prayers from a spirit-filled prayer warrior. I know it was the Holy Spirit operating in my father's life that led them straight to the accused. Without any doubt, the power of prayer and God's hand has been evident all of my life.

My father left for England when I was just shy of one year of age, and my mother followed him six months later leaving me in Jamaica to be raised by my loving grandmother, Ms. Eliza Smith, affectionately called "Ms. Liza" or "Sis"- by everyone in our community. The facts of life define her as my grandmother, but to me, she was 'my Mama,' the woman that raised me single-handedly. From what I am to understand, my grandparents had plans to marry, but my grandfather died before they were able to commit to matrimony. After his death, my grandmother made a decision not to get married, and she raised her children as a single mother.

Although my parents lived in England, my grandmother (whom I will refer to as my Mama for the remainder of this publication) made sure that I remembered that my parents existed. She never let me forget they were alive. My parents didn't write as often as they should have, but my Mama never said anything bad about them, nor did she criticise them. She never said that she was unhappy with them, nor did she make any judgments about them. Instead, she took care of me as if I were her own and made every effort to give me everything I needed. My Mama was a higgler (a person who buys and sells goods at the market), and the goods she sold allowed us to live a comfortable life. We did not have running water or electricity, but I collected wood to provide the fire for cooking. My Mama worked hard, and we had everything we needed; a roof over our heads, food to eat, and we had each other.

Years later, I learned that my Mama refused to release me to my birth-mother and held me as a ransom because she was scared she would never see her daughter again. By keeping me as a ransom, my Mama hoped to ensure that her daughter (my birth-mother) would come back to Jamaica and see her again. After learning this, I called myself "the ransom child." As clever as her ransom idea may have been, holding me as a ransom didn't work very well. I was a child when she left, and for over fourteen and a half years, it was just my Mama and me. Every now and then, Mama would open the doors of our home to help others in need, but for the most part, it was just she and I. Three days before my 16th birthday, I met my birth-parents for the first time at Heathrow Airport. I had a vague memory of what they looked like from an old photo framed on the wall. And on that day, it was as if I was meeting my birth-parents for the very first time. There I stood, at the airport, holding onto my suitcase and waited for what seemed like ages. I was awaiting their arrival, but honestly, I didn't know what the man and woman I was expecting to meet even looked like, and I didn't know how to greet them properly.

It was an awkward moment, but my Mama prepared me for my journey to England by giving me words of wisdom, *"A soft answer turns away wrath"* (Proverbs 15:1). She said, do not fuss and do not fret. From that day forward, I have always remained calm, and even to this day, I try not to shout; I do speak with a firm tone, but I never yell. My Mama wanted to make sure I looked my best to meet my parents, so she brought me to 44 Duke Street, Kingston, to have my first two-piece suit tailor-made for my trip. The suit cost me £25, and it was immaculate. Twenty-five pounds back then was a lot of money, but having a suit made to measure was worth it. She bought me a nice pair of shoes and gave me a passbook with £36 in it from selling the eggs and produce.

Finally, an announcement came over the speaker system, Mr. and Mrs. Brooks for Melvin Brooks! Not knowing who I would see, I held my suitcase with both hands until I heard a woman's voice say, "Hello, Son." I looked up and saw a couple, and after some deductive reasoning, I trusted that these were my parents, so I went along with them. Although I didn't know who they were, they had all the necessary documentation, letters, and a couple of photos sent in the past. The documents put us together, but this was not enough to develop a real connection between us. I knew that they were on one side of the world, in England, and I was over on the other side of the world in Jamaica, but there was no understanding of what that meant. They (my parents) had sent a wedding picture, but the photo did not help me identify them at all; they had changed over the years.

Leaving my Mama was nothing I wanted, desired, or even thought of. My father told me that he sent for me to unite with them in England because he heard I had begun to misbehave. I accepted his reason, but in my heart, I knew it wasn't the truth. I knew that no-one had written to report any misbehaviour because I never gave my Mama an ounce of trouble; I was a well-behaved boy who always listened. My entire life was surrounded by my Mama; I did not even have a girlfriend. Other than my Mama, cricket and dancing were my only loves. I was a well-respected boy; even my enemies respected me. I was honest and hard working. I did well in education and was offered an opportunity to attend construction school because my heart's desire was to become a builder. In fact, I was scheduled to begin attending classes that September in Maypen, Jamaica. Within eighteen months, I would have learned enough about building to start my trade, but of course, joining my parents in England changed everything. My father said the move was because of my behaviour, but I knew my behaviour could not have been the reason I had to leave Jamaica. The real reason was that my Mama was getting older and could no longer look after a young man growing up in Jamaica. I understood this, but I did not want to leave her.

I Remember Mama

Mama and I lived in a small district known as Tryall District. Our community was more like a small village with less than thirty houses filled with good families, and my Mama was loved by the community as a whole. I believe everyone loved my Mama because she had a very gentle and generous spirit. She was a Christian, a Baptist, who lived her life according to the Fruit of the Spirit, and everyone she came in contact with respected her. She was honest and always told the truth. Proverbs 31 describes her well. She was a very caring woman, and those who lived in the community looked to her for help all the time; she was an anchor to them. On occasion, when strangers who needed help came to town, people in the village would direct them to "go and see Ms. Liza, she will help you and tell her that I sent you!" She would take the strangers word that someone from the neighborhood sent them to her, and she would always lend money when asked, even if it was her last. Her kind nature was admirable as she looked after me and covered me so well that I never once missed my parents. She did her best to ensure that I had all I needed; yes, when times were hard, I went without, but even then, we always had enough. At Christmas time, she would give me a Christmas gift like a plastic whistle, an orange, or bun and cheese alongside a lovely breakfast of tomatoes, hot chocolate, and dumpling served with ackee and saltfish.

Today I have a good work ethic because my Mama taught me to work hard. She would take me into the field to harvest. She taught me to plant vegetables, pumpkins, tomatoes, etc. When they were harvested, she would take them to town and sell them. My Mama also raised pigs to sell to feed our family. Every Christmas, she would kill one, and we would eat a lot of it, so much so that I began to tire of pork and soon stopped eating it, and to this day, I still do not eat pork. Easter time, we would have

fish, hot cross buns and cheese, and sorrel drink, to name a few things. Weekly she would go to the market and sell stuff to buy things for our well-being. She would give me a hen, sell the eggs and save the money. Little did I know that she was saving the money from everything I produced just for me.

Without a doubt, I know My mama loved me dearly, and I loved her back. She was a beautiful lady who taught me everything about life, and she made sure I was capable of standing on my own two feet. She taught me as a young man to wash my clothes, iron, cook, mend my clothes, sew buttons, clean the house, look after the yard, etc. She taught me these valuable skills just in case the girl I married did not know how to do them, then I could help and teach her. Mama's way of thinking was a revelation to me because not many guys would marry a girl who could not already do these things, but my Mama's principle impacted my life. She said take what you know and teach someone else. Her philosophy gave me a desire to learn more so I could share more. I watched how she did things, and I imitated her. My Mama was an excellent cook, and she was able to make much from little. When we did not have meat in the house, she would take Chou-Chou (chayote), and she was able to cook it. She would crush it and mix salt fish in it, and it would be our meal for the day. She would make Jamaican Rundown from coconut and Mackerel, and my Mama made the best sweet potato pudding. Even now, in my mind, I can see her walking from the yard to the kitchen to put the pot on the fire, and whatever she put in that pot was going to be good!

My Mama never said too much to me about our finances, but I could tell things were getting pretty tough for her. There were times we were struggling, and my Mama could not afford to buy shoes for me to wear, so I walked around barefooted. I took care of my feet the same way other boys would take care of their special occasion shoes because my feet were my shoes. I always made sure that my feet were well oiled. I may have been barefooted, but I never had dry feet! Not many children had shoes in the village, so it was natural for us to walk around barefooted in the streets, to school, and even into town. My feet were my shoes, and I was never embarrassed. Knowing my Mama cared for me made up for any missing material possessions I did not own. My Mama was an industrious woman. She would help newly married couples that had no money earn the finances needed for their families. She would buy a cow and loan it to the couple until it produced. When the cow had its first calf, she would own one-third of its profits, and the couple would own two-thirds of its profits. When that cow would breed again, the couple would own half of the calf's profits, and she would own half of the profits. After the next breed, the birth of the third calf would be wholly owned by the couple. Once the third calf was weaned and grown, Mama would take back her cow and help someone else. She loved helping people, and she had such a creative mind, I have no idea where it came from.

Watching my Mama bless the lives of so many taught me so much and made me extremely proud of her. But at the same time, it hurt to see her help so many people, and those same people never return the favour when she was in need, as a boy that concerned me. My Mama had a heart made of gold. Regardless of how other people treated her, she never turned anyone away. Over time, our house was infested with woodworms, and it began deteriorating. I had to cut out the infected area and support it with other beams; the walls started to peel away, so I taught myself to do some patchwork and plaster them. You would think things couldn't get any worse, when in fact, they did. The roof in my room leaked, and when it rained, water came in, so I had to climb up and hold it together until Mama was able to get others to come and help us out. I didn't have a mattress, so I used old clothes as a mattress. There were times that we would not have any food in the house, and she would put water in a pot and put it on the fire and pray a prayer saying, "Dear

God, I beg you to send somebody with food for us!" I promise, by the time the pot nearly boiled out, we would hear someone at the bottom of our yard, calling, "Ms. Liza, Ms. Liza, send the boy down here!" Right there, her prayers were answered. The Lord would send someone with a basket of vegetables and food to give us. I believe the Lord blessed us because my Mama was a giver. She would cook the food others gave to bless us and share it with others in need like us. Everyone loved my Mama, and she was an excellent cook; everyone loved her food. I can equate her to Miss Marple: calm, patient, and kind. As you can imagine, our home was always open for fellowship and food.

As time moved on, Mama began to age but getting older didn't stop her from raising me with Christian discipline and instruction. There were only a few times I recall misbehaving. Once I misbehaved, and my Mama said, "wait, 'til I'll fix you." By midweek she had not yet done anything to me, which made me glad. I prayed that she would forget but no such luck, she remembered and came in saying, "You brute you, I'll catch you now," and I got a whooping! Mama would say, "wait until the cup runs over, then you will feel it; just wait until the cup runs over." Another time I remember she asked me something, and I responded in a way that was not polite, and she asked if she should lay down so I could beat her.

All in all, I was relatively a good child, but it was my love for cricket that got me in trouble. I loved playing cricket, and during the summertime, I would run off and play from sun up to sun down without ever telling my Mama where I had gone off to. Of course, this upset my

Mama, and she would say the famous saying of the Caribbean, "if you don't want to hear, you can feel." There were two occasions in my life where she called over our neighbor who lived on the hill to come over to give me a good smacking, and both times, I ran away. He was a good neighbor, but we later discovered he was a wicked man. He would beat his wife with a sybil jock. A sybil jock was a very flexible and bendable rod. Unfortunately, he used it regularly to beat his wife until she was black and blue. Because she was so fair in completion, the bruises were easily seen by everyone. I could never comprehend why a man would beat a woman? His actions angered me, and I wanted nothing to do with him. I knew I couldn't be in his company because I would hurt him for hurting her, so I ran away for a day. After daylight fell, I returned home to spend the night in the cellar. I realized my Mama was trying to teach me values by teaching me always to do the right thing. I am so grateful for every lesson learned.

Although my Mama taught me values, there was a time that temptation got the best of me, and I felt that as a young boy, I let her down big time. We had two ladies staying with us, one of which was bed-ridden and very ill, and the other lady was the caregiver who came over daily to take care of her. Our house was a two-roomed house consisting of only a living area and my Mama's bedroom. The living room was initially my room. It had a table, a cabinet, and a bed in the corner. To help our family members out, I had to give up my bed in the living room and share the bedroom with my Mama. During this time, I was around nine or ten years old.

Every Sabbath, Ms. Jess gave me an envelope that had her name, and the word tithes were written on the outside of it to take to church on her behalf. I had proven to be very trustworthy around money until one-day, temptation got a hold of me. I went into the room, and Aunt Clement had put two shillings on the cabinet. I never dreamt of taking anything and still can't believe I did. Those shiny silver coins were on the cabinet, and I took them, and I spent them. When Aunt Clement asked if anyone had seen them or removed them, I answered no. My mother asked me also, and I told her the same thing. Immediately I knew that I had lied and sinned, and for years, my error had an impression on my life. The disciplined boy was no longer disciplined. To this day, I can still see myself standing there, saying I never took them when I knew the entire time that not only did I take the coins, but I spent them. That turned my life a little bit as I recognized I lost my discipline. I did tell my Mama in the end, but I knew that something changed within me. I was tempted, and I yielded. This experience stayed with me for years. This memory's pain made me teach my children never to lie to me no matter how bad things are.

When I was about ten or eleven, Mama left to attend Convention and returned home with a horrible cough. My Mama's cough was so bad that she, in turn, became deaf. I can recall my Mama going to the doctor in Reed Mountain. The doctor was a good, wealthy doctor who gave her some rather large tablets that she probably paid what would be the equivalent of £70 in today's currency. Mama did as the doctor instructed, but she did not get any better. One day I came home from school, and I greeted her, but she did not answer, so I shouted my greeting at her in anger. I then realised how angry I was, but it was not that I was mad that she did not respond; it was the fact that she was sick. She had become deaf, and there was nothing I could do about it; I was helpless. But being deaf did not stop my Mama from helping others. She and I would go out into the plantations to help others with their crops. The boys in the plantations would laugh at my Mama for being deaf, and their laughter made me angry at her for being deaf. Her illness taught me a valuable life lesson, a person can be ill, and one can be angry about the illness, but you cannot take your anger out on the victim; there is nothing they can do to change their situation. This memory stayed with me for a while because of how I felt. My attitude towards her illness was terrible and showed immaturity. Her cousin from the country came to see her and gave me instructions to make a unique remedy. He instructed me to go to the coffee plantation and cut some bitter wood tree bark. I then had to take the bark and add some ganja (marijuana) for a special recipe that was then put to boil. He instructed me to boil four liters of the mixture until it evaporated to about one liter. The mixture was extremely bitter, so a little sugar was added to the recipe to make it taste better. Once the mixture cooled, it was then bottled.

The next morning Mama began drinking the formula; this was to be repeated for nine mornings. Mama took the mix for three days, and by the fourth day, she began releasing mucus and a substance that had a gritty texture. She began to cough up this black porridge-like substance from her body, it was gross, but we could tell the remedy was helping her.

As a matter of fact, I started drinking it too, and it cleared the spots on my body. By the seventh-day, Mama's hearing had been restored, she was completely cured by day nine, and my Mama could hear again. Thank God the remedy worked, but I definitely wouldn't recommend anyone trying this at home. The day that she could finally hear, I was overjoyed. Once our neighbors heard that she had gotten better, they invited us over for food and fellowship. We drank Porter and ate bread and rum cake. The music was good, and the food was even better. Of course, Mama and I were happy she could hear again, but so was everyone else.

I lived a good, unique life for a young boy, and I was well respected in our community. Other families in the community always wanted me to help them. The people around me were attracted to me because I was very gifted, talented, and willing to help others. So many people would ask my Mama's permission for me to go over to their houses to climb their apple or orange trees and pick their fruit for them so they could, in turn, sell them for wages at the market. People called upon me to help with all manner of things, but I was quiet and would often agree to be used without ever saying a word due to my speech impediment. Without hesitation, I would always do as I was told to help others, but sadly, no one ever gave me one dime. Those same people had children of their own, but they would send me, a ten-year-old, to watch over their ganja fields at night. I would sleep out in the fields by a tree to keep watch over the ganja plants. If anyone came to steal the plants, I would be there to stop them. Now when I think about it, I have no idea what I would have done if someone had come to steal them. When I think back to that time in my life, I wasn't thinking straight, and to this day, I have no idea why I went. I had no gun, no knife, and no machete, so what in the world would I have done if those big men would have come with guns and machetes? Had I been discovered, they would have killed me. After a long time, the thoughts of my actions has me in tears because when I think about it, the ganja crops were illegal, and I would have either been killed or arrested trying to help others who didn't even care enough about me to give me one dime for helping them. I was too young to realize it, but now, I am confident God had a purpose for my life because there is no way I should have survived. I was never the guy that would say no. I would always say yes when called upon, and looking back, saying "yes" was problematic. Watching the ganja was abuse because I was in danger of what could have happened while tending to their illegal ganja fields for free! My Mama would say, "never mind, son, God will bless you," but I developed my very own ideas about life over time. I saw things that I didn't like, and if given a chance, I would have changed my life for the better.

Although I was never paid a dime, on many occasions, Mama and I continued to help this same family, Mr. & Mrs. B. We didn't have telephones back then, so Mrs. B, who was an Adventist, would call up to my house by shouting as she walked past our home for me to come and help her with various chores that she could not handle alone. Sometimes my Mama would instruct me to stay with Mr. B. and his wife when she had to go out of town. She would leave on Thursday and come back home on Saturday night. Being the disciplined boy that I was, I would say yes, but I would never leave. I would stay home because I didn't like the way things were at Mr. & Mrs. B.'s house. They only had one bed in the room for all three of their kids to sleep in. Their kids were older than me, and they were bigger than me. I didn't like that, and I didn't like how they would use me while I was there, so I stayed home with my cousin. On Thursday night and Friday, I cooked for myself, cleaned the house, washed and ironed my clothes for school. Mrs. B. would pass by my house on Saturday to ask me to go to her home and cook dinner for her family. She felt I was available now that I no longer went to church regularly. So on Saturday afternoons, I cooked pea soup, dumplings, and yams for her family. I did all of this to keep myself busy. When Mama returned home, she didn't have anything to complain about; I had everything taken care of.

My Mama was the best thing that happened to me. She taught me life lessons that moulded and shaped me into the man that I am today, and those life lessons were a foundation for me to live my life pleasing unto God. She did not allow the shortcomings of my life to prevent me from excelling in life; my speech impediment, my stutter, my fast speaking, my left-hand condemnation, she never allowed any of those things to become excuses. She told me good manners would take me through the world, and I thought I could take my briefcase straight to Kingston airport and stand there with my head held high, ready to take on the world. In my heart, I truly believed that the principles my Mama taught me were more valuable than any amount of money, and armed with my passport in hand, I could go anywhere in the world and become the man I desired to be. I was not afraid of growing up. I took the principles she taught me and took charge of my life.

The last time that I saw my Mama was Sunday, 3rd October 1971. I arrived in Kingston to prepare to leave for England, but I had forgotten my passport at home. When I arrived back at the house to collect it, my Mama asked what was I doing back home? I explained to her that I had forgotten my passport. Just as I was leaving the second time, my Mama called me by my pet name and said, "When you get to England, be a good boy for your parents," I responded, "Yes, Mama," and I left and never looked back. I couldn't look back; I did as I was told to do. I went with Aunt Rita on the bus to the airport to meet my parents to travel back to England. Little did I know that Sunday, 3rd October 1971 would be the last time I would see my Mama. I left Jamaica at the age of 16 and never saw her again. On Monday 19th, January 1981, I received a telegram message that my Mama had died. The news shook me to the core, and I was devastated all the more because I could not attend her funeral. The wage earnings back in the 1980s were not lucrative enough to provide me with the funds to cover my rent and purchase a plane ticket to return to Jamaica. Losing my Mama was painful, and for years I cried because I could not attend her homegoing service. Without a doubt, I knew that Mama loved me, but it hurt to know that as much as she loved and cared for me, she would never see the man that I became or meet my wife and family. My heart desired to shower her with the love and support she deserved. When I think about all of the families she helped and how she invested so much into the lives of others, yet none of them reciprocated to show their appreciation to her near the end of her life, it saddens me. My Mama's house was left to me in her will, but after her death, instead of taking care of her home, her brothers tore it down and took all the materials, including the expensive cedar board stored in the basement. I was finally able to return to Jamaica in 1986 to visit her resting place. I later traveled back to Jamaica in 2004 and 2005. Each time I returned, it grieved me repeatedly that I never got back to see her before she went home to be with the Lord. She was a real gem; she never showed any difference; I was just her child. My Mama always said, "Choose your friends wisely because your friends are a reflection of yourself." I took her advice, and I believe I have chosen pretty well over the years.

Adopting other senior women as my grandmothers fills a massive void in my life. Spending time with them reminds me of all the great memories of my Mama. I am so grateful for these moments; somehow, it feels as if these moments compensate for the time that I missed spoiling my Mama before she went to be with the Lord. I love that I can spend time with women of wisdom and shower them with love and flowers. To this day, whether I am home or abroad, I always ask other families permission to spend quality time visiting with the elderly. I love to take my adopted grandmothers out for a nice dinner or an afternoon tea. The fellowship is always a blessing to me in so many ways. Like my Mama, I love children. Wherever I go, other family's children adopt me as their uncle or grandfather. My life is surrounded by the love and memories of my Mama. When I consider my then and my now, I am blessed, and I know it's because of my Mama. I realise that if it wasn't for the love of my Mama, my life could have been so different. So many of the young people I grew up with either went to jail or died before their time. My Mama balanced my thinking and made tremendous contributions to my development as a man and the husband, father, and Pastor that I am today.

II. My Mama's Pastor: Pastor Henry

Pastor Henry, my Mama's Pastor, was a prominent figure in developing me into the Pastor I am today. Pastor Henry was a vibrant, passionate, and convincing preacher. He only stood 5'2" in height, but he was tall in stature. He was the Minister of a prominent Baptist church in Spanish Town. Pastor Henry dressed in a neat suit, tie and hat and drove a Chevrolet to and from church every Sunday. I vividly remember the church because all the ladies wore white: white stockings, white shoes, white dresses, and white hats, and all the men wore black. We sat down in the crowd glued to every word that came out of his mouth while he preached from the balcony. He was a whooping preacher, and I thought, "WOW, this guy is small but powerful!" But I feared him. Pastor Henry scared the life out of me because, in my heart, I knew he heard directly from God. I believed he was a man sent by God to reveal if you were living in sin, and by what he said during that meeting, I felt like he could see directly in and through me!

He was a memorable man that made me fear to be in his presence. I can recall on one occasion, I was in the yard relaxing, and I saw him at a distance with his entourage coming towards my Mama's house. I realised that it was Pastor Henry, and immediately I did a life check to see if I had any sin, hidden or open within me. As he came closer to me, I stood up with my back straight and hands close to my side, almost as if I were called to attention. I knew he could see right through me; I froze and expected him to say, "Boy, you did ABC…," Although I could not recall committing any sins, I was sure I had. The impact of respect for a minister made me realise that people who are called to serve in the ministry play a significant role. The Word that a Minister speaks over the pulpit is life-changing. If a minister arrives at anyone's house, he should be received with respect. This Minister traveled quite a distance to visit our family, and that alone showed me how a Man of God serves the people of God. Pastor Henry had an excellent reputation, and the way my Mama loved and respected him changed my attitude; I still feared him, but I also revered him. I had a lot of respect for Pastor Henry, but I did not have a desire to become a minister. I knew exactly what I wanted out of life. I had made a plan for my life that consisted of five things: I wanted to go to a training school to become a builder, save up enough money to purchase land, build myself a house, buy a car, get married and become a committed Christian. That was my plan, and I wanted it to happen for me in that order. I wanted to own a Volkswagen to drive my family around in. I envisioned myself with my family having picnics with baskets of food and drinks, attending church together, sitting in the park, and just enjoying life as a family. Isn't that every man's dream?

My encounter with Pastor Henry was brief but impactful. He held a position of authority, and he knew exactly who he was and who he served. He was a compassionate leader. He didn't allow travel distance to stop him from seeing how my Mama and I were doing. To me, this was amazing and has helped shape my family and ministry life into what it is today. Pastor Henry impacted me with his preaching, how he lived his life, how he carried himself, and how he cared for the saints.

III. My First Head Teacher: Mr. Scott

At the age of 7, my mother's cousin and best friend, Icleyn Brown, brought me to school to begin my studies. One of my first teachers was a great teacher named Mr. Scott. He was a tiny light-skinned Cuban man who also stood about 5'2," but he was always dressed sharply and possessed undeniable charm. He was strong, assertive, skillful, an excellent teacher, and a great disciplinarian who so happens to be small and gifted. I loved his character and his stance. If you were late, you'd get the cane to your hand, and if you were not behaving in class, he would deal with you. He would jump from the podium to the table; Mr. Scott was no joke. I don't know why I liked him, but for some reason, I found him very intriguing UNTIL he got in trouble. Mr. Scott got a girl pregnant in school, and he had to be moved out. It upset me that he was leaving, but what he did was wrong, and he deserved to be punished for his crime. My encounter with Mr. Scott was brief, but it taught me that being a charming and handsome man has no bearings over right and wrong.

IV. My Subsequent Head Teacher:

Mrs. Merlyn V. Douglas

It wasn't long after Mr. Scott left that another teacher came to replace him. Mrs. Douglas arrived at school with an entourage, as if she was some kingpin! I gave her a hard time because, in my eyes, she was trying to take my teacher's place. Although I knew what Mr. Scott did was wrong, I was still upset and didn't want anyone taking his place. Mrs. Douglas didn't pay much mind to me; in fact, she paid me no attention at all. She did her role, and over time, she started drawing me close to her. I don't know why or how it happened, but I would occasionally accompany her to meetings. The evenings she travelled to Kingston, she would tell me I was going with her to town to take minutes or learn whatever she was doing. She took me everywhere she went. Sometimes I went alone, and other times she would invite this other young girl to come along with us. She had a beautiful Singer—a maroon Hillman Singer; it was a fantastic car with a fancy woodgrain dashboard. One day, we were going to town, and because a young lady was traveling with us, I thought I was not allowed to sit in the front seat, so I sat in the backseat. Mrs. Douglas then said to me, "you come and sit in the front seat; I'm not your chauffeur." From this, I learned that you only sit in the back seat of a car when the driver is chauffeuring you. If you're not a commuter, you sit in the front. I know it sounds simple, but for me, it was a fundamental principle to learn.

Over time we developed a great working relationship as student and teacher. She even trusted me with her school money. Once a month, she would give me the school's government cheque, and I would go to town to change it for her. I would walk all the way from school (the town was like Euston station back down to the M1) and go across the river with a leather briefcase held on top of my head. I would cross the river barefooted, with my trousers up and my shoes held in my hand. After I walked across the river, I would catch a bus to the Spanish Town where I would go to the bank to hand the cheques in. After I cashed the cheque, I would take the cash, put it in my briefcase and make the return journey: a bus back to the river, cross the river, then walk about a mile and a half back to school to give Mrs. Douglas the money. I repeated this errand once a month every month. Mrs. Douglas trusted me to do all of her errands. Whenever she needed help, she would call me; I was the one who she depended on. She taught me to strive for greatness. Once in class, we were doing English and Math lessons, and she noticed that I got all the answers to the questions right. Mrs. Douglas asked us to write down our signature, so I wrote my name and signed my signature (the one I use now). She looked at my signature and said, "one day you'll be a great man," and I believed her. Her words have stuck with me ever since that day.

Mama made enough money for the necessary things, but we still needed so much more. I had advanced in reading, writing, arithmetic, and learned to read drawings, which were the qualifications I was told that a builder must possess. So by the time I turned thirteen and a half, I decided to leave school to shadow my cousin as a builder. I worked alongside my cousin for about 18 months to learn enough about the trade to advance to builders school. At the age of fifteen, I tried to re-enter school, but I was told that I was too old to resume my schooling, so Mrs. Douglas made me the school's custodian. I took care of all the school's business; anything to do with repairs, that was my job. She made arrangements for me to enroll in an upcoming training school in May Pen to learn the ins and outs of building; her plan would have allowed me to work and train at the same time. But unfortunately, her idea did not come to fruition. I was to start training school in September, but a letter arrived from England informing me that I would be leaving Jamaica on 3rd October to go live in England. The news was a shock to us all. Mrs. Douglas did not want to see me leave, but she made sure I was well prepared for the move by organizing some summer work experience for me in Spanish Town at Mr. Chin's supermarket. Mrs. Douglas always had my best interest at heart.

England was a long way off from Jamaica, but distance did not hinder our relationship. Mrs. Douglas and I kept in touch until she went home to be with the Lord; she always spoke into my life and encouraged me to keep going and do the right thing. I wrote many letters to her, and I went back to her home to visit with her in Jamaica. The last time I saw her was in 2004. I was so disappointed when I found out that her first husband was unfaithful to her before he died; she did not deserve to be treated that way. She did remarry, but God as my witness, I don't know where in the world her mind was! She sold her house in the country and moved back to town in what I could only describe as a wooden garage. My heart broke to see where Mrs. Douglas was living. No woman as intellectual, extraordinary, and beautiful as she was should live in a shack. This house only had one bedroom and a little sitting area. She previously owned a big house in the country where the school was.

I can't remember what happened, but I heard there was a violent robbery, and she sold the house for little to nothing. When I arrived, I could not believe that she had lost everything, that broke me. Her finances were depleted, and she practically had nothing left. The man she married had nothing, and it was heartbreaking to see where she ended up in life. Time had begun to take a toll on her body. She was feeble, helpless, and could barely walk. I continued to write to her, send her money from time to time, and speak to her by phone whenever possible. I wish there were more I could have done for her. No sooner than I returned to England, I was informed that she had gone home to be with the Lord. I wish I could have attended her funeral service, but I had just left Jamaica, and I couldn't make another trip back to attend her funeral. However, I did write a tribute, and I asked a pastor friend of mine from a neighboring church to represent me by reading my written tribute at her funeral.

Mrs. Douglas was such an asset to my life. She helped shaped my life and the perception I had of myself. She said I was the only student in all her life that remembered her. Little did she know, there was no way in the world that I could forget her because of all of the amazing things she did for me. I wrote to her, visited her, and sent her money when she needed help because she had lost everything. Her second husband did

nothing to bring income into their home, and they were struggling day by day. I couldn't stand the thought of her living like this and did all I could to help her because she was good to me, and she was a constant influence in my life. She had no biological children, only; the child, her husband, had fathered outside of their marriage. And the amazing woman that she is, she loved and cared for the child regardless of the situation. I must say that Mrs. Douglas made a significant 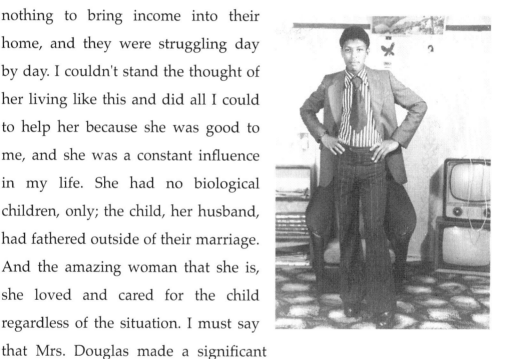 impact on my life. When my mother would go to Jamaica, my teacher would make sure she found her; she'd say, "I'm Mrs. Douglas, your son's former teacher, your son is a great man…" and she always spoke highly of me. Our relationship may have started off rocky, but Mrs. Douglas ignored that and recognized my potential from the moment she came to town, and she expected me to hold my worth.

My Mama impacted my life in ways indescribable. She gave me a spiritual foundation for my life. She taught me family, trust, calmness, love, and peace. My Mama introduced me to the concept of business, and my teachers continued her teachings by ensuring I understood the business side of life. Pastor Henry shaped my family and ministry life into what it is today. Although Mr. Scott disappointed me by getting a young girl pregnant, he still positively impacted my life. He was a positive, assertive, and direct man. He didn't play around, and that's what I liked about him. I admired his rules and learned the strength of leadership from him. Mrs. Douglas would take me to different places, which gave me exposure. She took me to business meetings in town and helped me develop responsibility and accountability. Can you imagine trusting a student from your school to cash your cheques for you? Today we wouldn't dare do that, and even back then, our ancestors had to think long and hard about it, but Mrs. Douglas trusted me! She would send me to collect money by the thousands. I never once got mugged, and I came back with every cent every time. I thank God for Mrs. Douglas's life, and I thank God that she took care of me. I can confidently say my grandmother's words and actions, the preacher, and my two teachers, Transformed My Life. Forever. Their influences began my transformation from A Disciplined Boy into a Man with a Message and a Ministry.

CHAPTER II

DISCIPLINE IS A LIFESTYLE

Discipline brings stability and structure into a person's life. It is the bridge between goals and accomplishment. The definition of the word discipline is dependent upon the context in which it is used. When used as a noun, discipline is defined to mean the practice of training people to obey rules or a code of behaviour. When discipline is used as a verb, it means to teach someone to follow the rules or a code of behaviour. The definition of discipline in my life transitioned as I embarked upon manhood. When my Mama informed the stranger that offered me the fruit that I was a *"disciplined boy,"* she meant that my son is raised to be mannerable and respectful. I carried my discipline into my adult life, and now I not only practice it, but I also teach it!

For me, discipline is a way of life. It's more than something I do; it is who I am. My strong spiritual upbringing moulded and shaped my life, and discipline was the centre of it. My Mama was a Proverbs 31 woman who built our family on the principles of God's Word. She was a woman of faith and a woman of prayer who used the Word of God as her "How To Manual." The Lord's Prayer, The Ten Commandments, and The Fruit of the Spirit were etched in her heart, and she taught me to love, live, honour, and obey God's Word. As a result of Mama's teaching, The Lord's Prayer became my line of communication with God, The Ten Commandments were the do's and don't's of my life, and the Fruit of the Spirit became my "What Would Jesus Do Guide." I honestly believe that I became so disciplined in my daily living because I watched my Mama work so hard to give me a good life, and I never wanted to disappoint her. Each one of my four role models profoundly influenced my life and helped to mould and shape me into a disciplined boy.

Your Life Is On Display

I didn't know it back then, but now I can identify the Fruit of the Spirit in each of my role models. In the New Testament, more than the Old, fruit is often understood symbolically as the product of either a good or evil life or an obedient or disobedient life. The fruit symbolises the consequence or product of repentance. The fruit of repentance toward God is, among other things, a change of attitude toward Him and His law. It represents the act of turning from being disobedient to His Word to being obedient to God's Word. The Apostle Paul penned the Fruits of the Spirit in the Epistle to the Galatians. Paul writes in Galatians 5:22-23: *"But the fruit of the Spirit is love, joy, peace, longsuffering, kindness, goodness, faithfulness, gentleness, self-control. Against such, there is no law."* These qualities or virtues are produced by the action of the Holy Spirit in us. They grow in a person who, by faith, obeys God's Word through the guidance and power of God's Spirit. Elements of this equation must be used to produce the right fruit—God's Word, His Spirit, faith, and obedience to God's Word. These, along with some others, produce significant fruits of righteousness.

Christians who have been given the Holy Spirit have the opportunity to become walking billboards and tell the world of God's existence and wisdom. When we demonstrate the fruit of the Spirit, people watch and take notice. Neither one of my mentors ever uttered the words, "pay attention to how I live." In fact, their walk did all the talking, and neither one of them ever had to say anything at all, yet their fruit was evident in how they lived their lives. Every day their lives were on display. I watched each one of them in action and decided to become a billboard for Jesus Christ.

The Fruit of the Spirit

The following biblical attributes were seen in their day to day walk:

I. Love — Much like the word discipline, love can either be a noun or a verb depending on its context. Here in the text, the word love is not referring to feelings but more of a decision of goodwill and devotion to others. Love gives freely without looking at whether the other person deserves it, and it gives without expecting anything back.

I could see love operating in each of my mentors. My Mama showed me love daily by providing for me and going above and beyond to make ends meet, even when she had to create the ends. As busy as Pastor Henry was, love made him stop by and check on Mama and me. He didn't have to do it, but love made him do it. Mr. Scott displayed love through his consistency as a disciplinarian. Even when I made every attempt not to like Mrs. Douglas, she won me over by loving me despite how I initially treated her.

II. Joy — People often mistake joy for happiness or may use them interchangeably. Joy, as described in Galatians, speaks of a 'calm delight' that is entirely independent of whether life is going good or bad. Joy denotes a supernatural gladness of the Holy Spirit present even during the storms of life, and often more so during these times. This type of joy can only be present when a person can focus on how God creates purpose out of pain, rather than focusing on the pain itself.

Life presented some pretty hard times for my Mama, yet instead of griping and complaining, she played the cards she was dealt and never allowed the enemy to steal her joy. There were times when our cupboard wasn't just bare; it was downright empty. But an empty cupboard couldn't steal Mama's joy. She would sing to the tune of expectation as she boiled a pot of water, waiting to see who God would send to the house with food for us to eat. She found that unspeakable joy because she knew the God she served was an on-time God.

III. Peace — It is no good just hoping that a chaotic situation will go away, but what will be beneficial is finding peace in the midst of the madness. Similar to joy, peace is that contentment knowing that God has the situation in His hands.

Our reaction to the events that unfold in our lives often serves as the thermostat to the outcome. The believer who places his or her full confidence in a loving God and is thankful in every circumstance controls the power to possess supernatural peace. He gives us peace that is an inner calm that dominates the heart. It may appear that everything surrounding you is falling apart, but there is something on the inside that is not moved by what is seen by the physical eye. To most, it will remain a mystery how someone can be so serene in the midst of turmoil. Somehow, a bad cough led to my Mama becoming deaf, and although she was talked about, ridiculed, and mistreated, she remained at peace with God and confident that He would make her whole again in His time.

IV. Longsuffering — Other words that describe this fruit are patience, forbearance, perseverance, and steadfastness. It is the ability to endure ill-treatment from life or at the hands of others without lashing out or paying back.

I never understood how or why my Mama would continue to help the same people over and again that never extended a hand when she was down, but she did. She had a heart made of gold, and regardless of how other people treated her, she never turned anyone away that needed her help. My Mama had this NEVER Quit, NEVER Give-up spirit. Any commitment she made, she maintained and completed her mission to the end.

V. Kindness — When kindness is at work in a person's life, they look for ways to adapt to meet others' needs. It is moral goodness that overflows. It is also the absence of malice.

On countless occasions, my kindness was taken for weakness. So many people would ask my Mama's permission for me to go over to their homes, climb their apple or orange trees and pick their fruit for them so they could, in turn, sell their fruit for wages at the market. There were times I risked my life to watch ganja plants and was never offered one dime. It bothered me that my hard work and value were overlooked, but my Mama would say, "never mind, son, God will bless you." She taught me that even when others do not see your value, God does, and He will rightly reward you.

VI. **Goodness** — While kindness is the soft side of good, goodness reflects the character of God. The goodness in you desires to see the goodness in others.

Each of my mentors displayed goodness not just from the words that flowed from their lips, but I could also see the goodness in their daily walk. My Mama had an honourable reputation within the community in which we lived. The community as a whole loved my Mama because she was a good woman; she helped everyone. The neighbours, the newlyweds, the church, and even the strangers in town; only good people help strangers. My encounter with Mrs. Douglas allowed me to see how a stranger could demonstrate goodness to someone they don't know. When Mrs. Douglas took Mr. Scott's position as my headteacher, I resented her. Yet, regardless of my behaviour towards her, Mrs. Douglas saw something in me and did not allow my actions to hinder my blessings. Her actions changed my life forever.

VII. **Faithfulness** — A faithful person, is one with real integrity. He or she is someone others can look to as an example and one genuinely devoted to others and Christ. Our natural self always wants to be in charge, but Spirit-controlled faithfulness is evident in the life of a person who seeks good for others and glory for God.

Pastor Henry impacted me with his preaching, how he lived his life, and how he carried himself. Pastor Henry held a position of authority, and he knew exactly who he was and who he served. I watched how others respected him and how the words he spoke were life-changing to the ears it fell upon. Growing up, I never desired to be a minister, but now I know the Lord had Pastor Henry in my life so I could see a faithful Man of God providing good for others and doing it all for the glory of God.

VIII. Gentleness — Meekness does not mean weakness. Gentleness is not lacking in power. Gentleness always forgives others, always corrects with kindness, and always lives in tranquility.

I've always heard grandparents say that the love for a grandchild is in no comparison to the love of a birth child. I honestly did not understand this until I became a grandfather myself. The Lord blessed me with my first granddaughter, Jade Zara Lee Linton, and it's like I had a heart transplant without undergoing surgery. Her existence increased the size of my heart, and the expansion she created is a space that is moulded just for her. I never understood how my grandmother could love me so much until now.

My Mama wasn't a young woman when my parents left for England, but she never allowed her age to hinder her ability to care for me. She raised me with Christian discipline, instruction, and love. I was never a bad child, but there were times when I was a handful; I was a growing boy. Once she asked me something, I responded in a way that was not polite, and she asked if she should lay down so I could beat her. If I ever deserved a backhand, speaking disrespectfully to my Mama was reason enough for it. However, she disciplined me with love. She was always gentle in her approach, and her actions taught me to be quick to listen, slow to speak, and slow to become angry. She was as gentle as a lamb.

IX. Self-control — In Romans 7, Paul speaks of the flesh being continually at odds with the spirit and always wanting to dominate. Self-control is releasing our grip on what the flesh desires and instead choosing to be led by the Holy Spirit. It is power focused in the right place.

My brief encounter with Mr. Scott provided me with one of my greatest life lessons. When I met Mr. Scott, I looked up to him and admired him. He was always dressed sharply and possessed undeniable charm. Mr. Scott was tiny, but he was strong, bold, confident, orderly, and a great disciplinarian. I loved his character and his stance. When I first met him, I wanted to be just like him until I learned of his actions. Yes, he was a handsome, stern, charming man that dressed well, but none of that had any bearings over right and wrong. There is absolutely nothing right about a grown man violating and impregnating a student entrusted to his care. Great men of God honour and uphold the values of Christianity. Mr. Scott's errors taught me the importance of self-control. The topic of "self-control" does give an implication that one emerges in a battle between a divided self. This battle of control begins when our "self" produces desires we should not satisfy but instead "control." We should deny ourselves and take up our cross daily, Jesus says, and follow him (Luke

9:23). Daily our "self" produces desires that should be "denied" or "controlled" to please God.

The Holy Spirit Is the Source of Our Fruit

The Apostle Paul names these nine biblical attributes as the Fruit of the Spirit. The attributes are written in a singular form, indicating that we should understand that the fruit has many components, but at the same time, all of them will be produced within each person as the Spirit leads. Paul pointedly drew attention to the source of the fruit as being "of the Spirit" to make us fully aware that these attributes do not flow from our natures. The "works of the flesh" listed in Galatians 5:19-21 are the product of our human heart. But the spiritual fruit is produced through the Holy Spirit. Even after conversion, our heart is not the source of this spiritual fruit.

The nine biblical attributes can be divided into three general groups, with each group consisting of three qualities. Of course, we can expect some overlapping of application between the three groups:

A. The first group—love, joy, and peace—portrays a Christian's mind in its most general aspect with particular emphasis on one's relationship with God.

B. The second group—longsuffering (patience), kindness, and goodness—contains social virtues relating to our thoughts and actions toward fellow man.

C. The final group—faithfulness (fidelity), gentleness, and self-control—reveals how a Christian should be in himself with overtones of his spiritual and moral reliability.

All three groups possess qualities we should have a great desire for. Without them, we cannot rightly reflect the mind and way of God. When we follow the Spirit's lead instead of being led by our self-focused desires, He produces the fruit. But even when we don't walk by the Spirit, He is the very one who convicts us that things are not in proper order in our lives. God promises that if we are willing to admit that we have been walking our own way and ask for His forgiveness and cleansing, He will empower us through His Spirit to live above ourselves and live the abundant life for which He has created us. The fruit of the Spirit reflects the virtues God would manifest before humanity. Seeking first the Kingdom of God and His righteousness through yielding to His Word will produce these characteristics of God in us. Then, as we become like Christ, we will, like Him, glorify God.

CHAPTER III

DISCIPLINE TRANSFORMED

MY MANHOOD

A man's transition into manhood differs from one individual to the next, and the change begins with each man's definition of manhood. Even the definition of 'manhood' within itself is defined in various ways. Finding a clear and precise definition of masculinity is especially difficult if we turn to the world rather than the Bible. "Ultimately and completely, masculinity is defined by the God who makes men." God sent His only Son, Jesus, as the perfect divine depiction of manhood. Jesus is the definition of true masculinity. In looking at the life of Jesus, every man can find countless attributes and commitments that show us how to live as a man faithful to the Father's call. The truth of the matter is: you're not a man until you learn to act like one. It should be every man's mission in life to be more like the greatest model of manhood, Jesus Christ. Transforming to be more like Him is a process, and it begins with the nine biblical attributes of the Fruit of the Spirit.

At the age of 16, I immigrated to England to join my family in Stafford, and immediately upon my arrival, I had to show my manhood. I instantly became the big brother to my siblings, and at times it became necessary to show the English striplings who was the boss. The Fish and Chips lads didn't stand a chance against this Jamaican Yam and Dumpling. It wasn't long before everyone saw how good I was at cricket, and I began playing in the county of Staffordshire. I was able to enjoy the game I loved while holding down a job at GEC Measurements, where I quickly processed through the ranks to the position of a Store Controller. I played for Stafford, Lotus Shoes, and GEC Measurements, where I was spotted and encouraged to go for a trial at Warwickshire Cricket Club. I loved the game, but accepting the commitment to play for Warwickshire County would interfere with my obligations to my church, particularly

my responsibilities to the Youth Service, because I really loved helping with the Youth Services. As much as I enjoyed playing cricket, it was in no comparison to how amazing it felt to serve others. My father needed my help driving the church bus, and helping my earthly father was helping my heavenly Father. With no regrets, I left cricket behind and gave my all to serve God and His people.

My father was the Pastor of Mount Peniel Church in Wolverhampton, and soon after my arrival in England, I immediately begin attending church with my family. It wasn't long before I was fully immersed in church life. The church needed someone to drive the bus, so I just did it. My greatest desire was to serve and help meet others' needs, so I served wherever I saw unmet needs. I never waited for someone to ask me to do anything; I just did it. Without being given the title of a Deacon, I began serving in the capacity of one. I honestly believe that as I was serving, the call God had on my life intensified. Although others could see the call in me, I could not. Over time, I was given the charge as a Deacon and served the Body of Christ for the Glory of God. When I look back over my life, it amazes me to see how the Lord was preparing me for His service my whole life.

Little did I know that when my Mama spoke the words, "*He is a disciplined boy,*" she wasn't just defining my character; she was also speaking words of prophecy over my life. I was almost five thousand miles away from her, but daily I could hear her voice say those five words, and my every decision was centred around "*He is a disciplined boy.*" I knew she couldn't physically see me, but a huge part of me believed her eyes were always upon me, and there is nothing that I would ever do to disappoint my Mama.

Again, I can't recall when it happened, but I was transformed into a man. The time had come for me to fulfill the five-point plan I set for my life: I wanted to go to a training school to become a builder, save up enough money to purchase land and build myself a house, buy a car, get married and become a committed Christian. I desired to live a life pleasing to God with a wife and family, and my five-point plan was the foundation I set for my life. I made a decision to become a husband, and I centred my decision around Ephesians 5:25. "*Husbands, love your wives, even as Christ also loved the church, and gave himself for it.*" The Word of the Lord declares, "*He who finds a wife finds a good thing, And obtains favor from the Lord,*" Proverbs 18:22.

I found my good thing, my gift in the person of Yvonne Elizabeth Clarke.

God's Divine Order for Family

Understanding God's divine order for the family was one of the greatest assets to my development as a man. I believe God's hierarchy of family order is: God the Father, Jesus Christ, husband, wife, and children, in that order. My belief is nothing I made up. His Word is the foundation of my understanding. I Corinthians 11:3 reads, *"But I would have you know, that the head of every man is Christ; and the head of the woman is the man; and the head of Christ is God."* One of the best examples to demonstrate God's divine order for the family is the "Umbrella of Authority" concept. This concept has been around for many years and taught in Bible studies worldwide. Here's an illustration to help enhance your thought process:

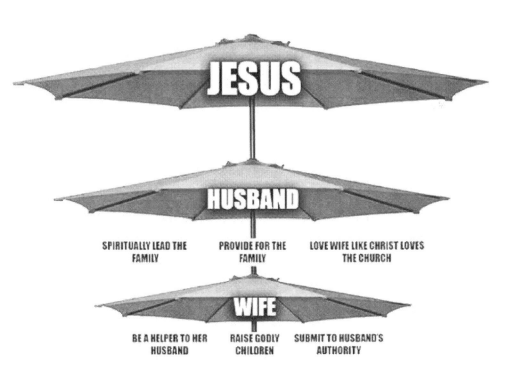

Ephesians 5:23 reminds us that *"the husband is head of his wife as Christ is head of the church."* According to scripture, I have a responsibility to be the head of my family, and this authority is sacred. Being the head does not mean that my family lives under dictatorship ruling or tyranny, but it does mean that the Lord holds me accountable for the decisions that I make for my family. Although I have the last say when it comes to making decisions for my family, it is my responsibility to consider my wife and my children's needs and desires to lead and direct my decision-making. As the leader of my family, I have to make decisions for the good of the whole group. Before making any decision, to this day, I always take the time to talk to my wife and children to get a clear understanding of their wants, desires, and views on any subject.

I believe there are four essential rules for building God's family. The rules are simple:

1. Wives must submit to their husband's authority.
2. Husbands are to love their wives and not be harsh with them.
3. Children must obey their parents in everything.
4. Parents are not to aggravate their children.

As a man of God, I dedicated every fibre of my being to follow God's design and build my family in divine order.

Understanding Family, Church and God's Authority

God's idea of family was introduced at the very beginning of time. Genesis 1:28, *"God blessed them and said to them, 'Be fruitful and increase in number; fill the earth and subdue it. Rule over the fish of the sea and the birds of the air and over every living creature that moves on the ground.'"* God's plan for creation was for men and women to marry and have children. A man and a woman would form a "one-flesh" union through marriage (Genesis 2:24). They, with their children, become a family, the essential building block of human society. The family is the most critical building block of human society, and as such, it should be nurtured and protected.

The family unit is a duplicate of another establishment God has ordained—the church. Jesus Christ is the head of the church. He is the authority. The church, as a whole, is His bride. We, as individuals in the church, are His children and siblings, one with another.

Family provides children with a better understanding of God, His church, and His authority. If your children never learn to respect their parents, whom they live with, and interact with, how will they learn to respect God whom they cannot see? When parents teach their children the importance of authority, responsibility, and consequences for wrong actions, they will much more quickly understand who God is and the authority He has in our lives.

Every responsible man must know that the family is considered the backbone of society. Think about it, after a child is born, he/she is entirely dependent upon his family for everything. After birth, it is the family's responsibility to provide shelter, food, clothing, love, affection, and security. The best model for the family is the church. It's up to the parents to provide their children with an excellent example of how to live a Christian life and teach them about love, companionship, and forgiveness. It's within the family, a child learns right from wrong and provides opportunities for entertainment and enjoyment.

Understanding The Roles & Responsibilities of Each Family Member

God has chosen the family's framework to help us understand authority and His plan for our lives. The family institution is nothing new; God instituted the family in Genesis 2:18 when He said, *"It is not good that the man should be alone; I will make him an help meet for him."* He then formed Eve from a rib of Adam as told in verses 21-24, *"This is now bone of my bones, and flesh of my flesh: she shall be called Woman, because she was taken out of Man. Therefore shall a man leave his father and his mother, and shall cleave unto his wife: and they shall be one flesh."*

God brought Adam and Eve together and established the basis for the family. This basis is a man and a woman. Although Adam and Eve did not have parents, God instituted at that time the principle that a man and woman would depart from their parents and family unit as they once knew it to begin a new family unit.

According to scripture, there is no family without a man and a woman uniting together in marriage.

God's desire for the family is to reproduce and multiply. God desires that husbands and wives bring forth offspring; reproduction is

God's definition for a family. Genesis 1:27 and 28 says, *"So God created man in his own image, in the image of God created he him; male and female created he them. And God blessed them, and God said unto them, Be fruitful, and multiply, and replenish the earth, and subdue it: and have dominion over the fish of the sea, and over the fowl of the air, and over every living thing that moveth upon the earth."*

Within the family, God has given its members roles and responsibilities:

A. Husband

Ephesians 5:25-28: *"Husbands, love your wives, even as Christ also loved the church, and gave himself for it; That he might sanctify and cleanse it with the washing of water by the word, That he might present it to himself a glorious church, not having spot, or wrinkle, or any such thing; but that it should be holy and without blemish. So ought men to love their wives as their own bodies. He that loveth his wife loveth himself."*

God commands husbands to love their wives as their own flesh. When a man does not love his wife as he should, he does not fulfill God's plan as the family's husband and father.

B. Father

Ephesians 6:4: *"And, ye fathers, provoke not your children to wrath: but bring them up in the nurture and admonition of the Lord."*

By definition, a father is a man who has begotten a child. This verse tells us that fathers are to bring up their children in the teachings of the Lord and not "provoke them to wrath" or badger and shame them until they hate their father.

C. Wife

Ephesians 5:22, 23: *"Wives, submit yourselves unto your own husbands, as unto the Lord. For the husband is the head of the wife, even as Christ is the head of the church: and he is the savior of the body."*

Wives are told to submit to their husbands. When a wife submits to and respects her husband's authority, it helps the children understand their need to submit to the authority over them.

D. Mother

1 Timothy 5:14: *"I will therefore that the younger women marry, bear children, guide the house, give none occasion to the adversary to speak reproachfully."*

Titus 2:4, 5: *"That they may teach the young women to be sober, to love their husbands, to love their children, To be discreet, chaste, keepers at home, good, obedient to their own husbands, that the word of God be not blasphemed."*

Young mothers are taught by the older women in the church to bear children, love their husbands, guide the home, obey, submit, and educate their children. By doing so, their children will grow up being taught to honour God's Word.

E. Children

Exodus 20:12: *"Honour thy father and thy mother: that thy days may* be long upon the land which the LORD thy God giveth thee."

Ephesians 6:1-3: *"Children, obey your parents in the Lord: for this is right. Honour thy father and mother; which is the first commandment with promise; That it may be well with thee, and thou mayest live long on the earth."*

Children are to obey and honour their parents. This command means that children need to obey and be obedient in a respectful way that adds value to the family unit and their parents. The Bible teaches that those who honour their parents will live longer lives than they would if they were disobedient, hateful, and disrespectful to their mother and father.

My Gift

Stored in my mental cabinet of values were two incidents where I witnessed the vows made to God to love, comfort, honour, and keep your spouse for as long as you both shall live shattered like broken glass. I have a memory of seeing black and blue bruises all over the body of a young lady in our community because her wicked husband beat her with a sybil jock. As a young man, that hurt me. Witnessing this first hand served as a reminder of what never to do. And, I can recall watching the wife of another man within our community stroll through town with her boyfriend locked in her arms while her husband was away working to provide for his family. That also hurt me. Witnessing this first hand served as a reminder of what never to tolerate. My desire for marriage was nothing like what either of these men was producing or tolerating.

In addition to desiring a beautiful, smart woman, I wanted a wife that loved the Lord and would push me to be my best self. A wise man desires a woman with ideas, skills, hopes, plans, and dreams—a whole panorama of abilities she brings to the marriage. Having a wife with these characteristics is vital because, in many areas, the husband is dependent upon her knowledge, insight, courage, faith, and expertise. The Lord blessed me with everything I desired and more. He blessed me with my tailor-made gift, Yvonne Elizabeth Clarke.

Yvonne had it all, and I wanted her to be my wife. She was smart, beautiful, kind, gentle, a woman of faith, and she had a sense of humour that excited me. To this day, no matter what we are faced with, Yvonne can see the bright side of everything, and somehow, she always has confidence in me, and that is so sexy to me. One of the qualities of "the wife of noble character" described in Proverbs 31 is that (v. 25, NIV). Along with this ability, the passage explains that she is tender but also tough. She can oversee numerous projects and handle all the variables. When the threat of discouragement or destruction looms, she can chuckle to herself because her dependence is upon God.

My Family

Yvonne and I are dynamic together; we are a team. She and I have created a partnership consisting of two people working together toward the same vision in support and love. Her grace and strength always compensate for my lack and weaknesses. The Lord has blessed us with a beautiful family. We have three amazing and gifted children: Rebecca, Adam, and Matthew. Rebecca is our oldest and only daughter, who has one of the most anointed voices in the world. Many call Rebecca, The Voice! Her gift is AMAZING! Adam, our middle child and first son, is known to many as 'The Maestro.' The anointing he carries transfers through his fingers, and the melodies he plays on the keyboard shifts the atmosphere to a point where you can feel it. His gift is AMAZING! Matthew, our youngest child, shares his gifts and talents across the nation. If you put a set of drumsticks in the 'Beat Master's' hands, the beat never stops! His gift is AMAZING! No, I have not overused the word AMAZING; it is what it is. The Lord has done an AMAZING work in our lives, and I'm glad about it.

My Family - My Responsibility

My five-point plan became my family's five-point plan. We prayed about it, put our trust in God, and the Lord provided an increase. Yvonne and I are an incredible team, but according to scripture, I know that as the man, my family is ultimately my responsibility; I am the head of my household. Being the head of your family is not about having the upper hand, nor is it to mean that a woman has no rights or is a second-class citizen. On the contrary, God gives the husband some very severe commands: *"Husbands, love your wives, just as Christ also loved the church and gave Himself up for her; that He might sanctify her, having cleansed her by the washing of water with the Word, that He might present to Himself the church in all her glory, having no spot or wrinkle or any such thing; but that she should be holy and blameless"* (Ephesians 5:25-27). Headship is more about order and not about saying one person is better or more important. The husband is the head of the wife in the family, and he has the responsibility of guiding his family to a closer relationship with the Lord. God will require it of him on the day when God judges all our deeds. Being a man is not all about masculinity, but manhood is exhibited in one's responsibility to his wife and children.

Being a man is not about being the one who gives orders in your house or paying the bills; a boy can give orders and pay bills. Manhood is defined by a man's commitment to being present and influential in the lives of those people who matter most to him, his family.

I have summed up five critical responsibilities a man has to his family:

I. Be A Priest In His Home -

In good times and bad times, the man should know that his family is looking to him for direction and leadership. It is the man's responsibility to lead his family according to the Word of God. He must lead his family to the house of worship and live a life of worship by leading the reading of scripture, family prayer, and praying over his family at home.

II. Be A Prophet To His Family -

A responsible man sees the potential in his family members and speaks God's favour over their lives. In the same manner, he sees the weakness in those he loves and encourages and helps them overcome their shortcomings. If a man has to correct, he should always do this with love and never curse. *"Death and life are in the power of the tongue"* (Proverbs 18:21), and a responsible man knows that his tongue can make his marriage sweet, his family strong, and his church healthy. Tongues can give hope to the despairing, advance understanding, and spread the gospel. However, the same tongue can also be the death of marriages, families, friendships, churches, careers, hopes, understanding, reputations, missionary efforts, and governments. It all boils down to what's filling your heart. Jesus said, *"Out of the abundance of the heart [the] mouth speaks"* (Luke 6:45). A critical heart produces a critical tongue. A self-righteous heart produces a judgmental tongue. A bitter heart produces a malicious tongue. An ungrateful heart produces a grumbling tongue. But a loving heart produces a gracious tongue. A faithful heart produces a truthful tongue. A peaceful heart produces a reconciling tongue. A trusting heart produces an encouraging tongue. Men, what are you speaking into the life of your family?

III. Be the Provider for His Family -

A responsible man understands that a call to marriage is a call to accept the divine role as the provider for his family. He works hard to ensure that his family's needs are met and goes beyond today's requirements and plans for tomorrow's needs. He teaches his family to plan, save, and invest for the future.

It is essential that men understand that providing for their family means more than meeting physical needs. It also means taking responsibility to provide for emotional and spiritual needs. A father should teach his children and prepare them to become responsible adults who, in turn, teach the same principles to their family.

IV. Be the Protector of His Family -

God has given men greater physical strength than women and has also given men a need or desire to be protectors. A responsible man uses his God-given strength to protect his wife and children at all costs. Not only does he protect his family from danger, but he defends them emotionally, spiritually, from sin and financial ruin.

V. Be Present and Involved In His Family's Life -

God has given the man a unique and special role to function for his family in the reflection of Jesus Christ Himself. A responsible man takes pride in fulfilling his role as a husband and a father and his charge to nurture and care for every family member. He remains faithful to his responsibilities and never runs away from his duties. Instead, he finds strength in his disciplined lifestyle and joy in keeping the commandments of God to raise his family to live by the Fruit of the Spirit.

What a tremendous honour and responsibility it is to have the role of father and husband!

My Next Move

It's hard to pinpoint when it happens, but, in the course of every man's life, he has this kind of "a-ha" moment; it's that moment of sudden insight or discovery. The moment he realises, "Oh My God," I am responsible for the lives of my family. Some men experience it while driving alone in the car, trying to find solutions to better their family. Some realise it after returning home from their honeymoon. For some, it happens the second the life he has created is placed in his hands. My five-point plan had come to fruition, and the total outcome of my plan was dependent upon my next move.

When a boy transforms into a man, he does not receive a magic manual of manhood. Unfortunately, no how-to guide is available to provide step-by-step instructions on what a man is to do. As a man, it was my responsibility to lead my family. As the priest/prophet of my home, I realised I was responsible for setting the guidelines and parameters to protect and provide for my family. The words I AM RESPONSIBLE are serious and, to some degree, can be very scary. Not only did my family depend on me, but God also depended on me. It was my responsibility to provide my family with a fair start in life by building a firm foundation for them to build their lives upon. I didn't have all of the answers, but I did have a disciplined life to start my building process. My Mama's labour of love would not go in vain. Every prayer she prayed, every lesson she taught me, and every value she instilled within me prepared me for this moment in my life: manhood. God strategically prepared my journey into manhood. My God would become their God; my values would become their values; they would believe what I believed; their everything was dependent upon me. My family depended on me to take a huge step of faith and trust God to be my everything.

As fearful as taking that step of faith may be, we find both comfort and confidence in knowing that with God on our side, we will not fail. King David penned the 37th Psalm to remind the reader of their place in the universe. His words remind us that God's plan for our lives will come to fruition; it's up to the good man to take a step in the right direction. The encouraging words of the text, *"The steps of a good man are ordered by the Lord: and he delighteth in his way,"* gives us the strength to be the men our families need us to be. By His grace and Holy Spirit, the Lord directs the thoughts, affections, and designs of good men. When we confess that He is our God, we can find strength in knowing that he holds the hearts of good men in the hollow of His hands, and he will oversee every event that concerns every good man and his family. He promises to get ahead of us and clear the pathway in the lives of our family. Every good man can find strength in knowing that when the Lord covers him, He is also covering his family, and He promises to lead, guide, and direct our every step. God orders the steps of a good man, not only by His written word but by whispering into his conscious man, saying, This is the way, walk in it. He does not always show His way at a distance, but he leads us step by step, as children are led, to keep us in continual dependence upon His guidance.

Turn left or turn right, go forward or turn around and return where you came from, spend the light bill money or buy groceries, say yes to the sleepover, or let your children think you're the meanest father on the earth. Decisions, decisions, decisions, what is a man to do? As tough as the decision-making process can be, every man must take a step of faith and trust God to be there as his safety net. Every step that we take is a step that says I trust God to be there for my family and me. Matthew Chapter 14 recounts one of the many miracles of Jesus following the miracle of him feeding the five thousand. At the end of the evening, the disciples got into a ship to cross to the other side of the Sea of Galilee, without Jesus, who went up the mountain to pray alone. During the journey on the sea, the disciples were distressed by the wind and the waves but saw Jesus walking towards them on the sea. The disciples were startled to see Jesus, but he told them not to be afraid. *"And Peter answered him and said, Lord, if it be thou, bid me come unto thee on the water"* (Matthew 14:28). After Peter came down out of the ship and walked on water, he became afraid of the storm and began to sink. *"But when he saw the wind boisterous, he was afraid; and beginning to sink, he cried, saying, Lord, save* me. And immediately, Jesus stretched forth his hand, and caught him, and said unto him, O thou of little faith, wherefore didst thou doubt?" (Matthew 14:30-31).

Has this ever happened to you? Have you ever heard the voice of God, took a step of faith to do what God told you to do, only to retract and second-guess his command? Sure you have, we all have. Your wife has been asking for a new refrigerator, and finally, you make the decision to purchase it for her. As soon as you get it home, the boiler goes out, and your son walks in with a note from school requesting £250 for summer camp. Here's your first thought, Why didn't I wait and purchase the refrigerator later? For some reason, doubt is always our first response. Instead of doubting God, we must learn to trust every command that God gives us. Just like flying darts, life will present circumstance after circumstance, and the outcome is dependent upon your initial decision to trust God and believe that He always makes a way out of no way. At the moment, you may feel like your back is against the wall, but here's what you don't know. Yes, the purchase of the refrigerator was a huge expense, and although your bank account does not have the funds to repair the boiler or the £250 for your son's summer camp, you don't need the money. Why aren't the funds needed? Because the Lord has already made a way out of no way. One of the men from your church calls you out of the blue, and guess what, he is a certified plumber. He comes over to repair your boiler at no cost to you, and during a casual conversation, you ask one simple question, How is your wife doing? That one question led him to share his family's exciting news. His wife, the principal of your son's school, just received grant funding for the school's summer camp program, and he asks if you know of any students that may be interested in attending? Has anything like this ever happened to you? Any way you look at it, the decision-making process is difficult, and making decisions for your family is never easy. Just when you think you have made the right decision, you are faced with something else.

Here are seven essential decision-making steps that stand out from this passage. I believe these steps will help the responsible man in making decisions for himself and his family:

I. Don't be afraid. Regardless of the situation, do not allow fear to overtake you.

II. Tell God all about it. Whatever it is you need, ask the Lord for it. *"Ask, and it shall be given."*

III. Don't move until you hear from God. Make sure all of your green lights are coming from God and no one else.

IV. Trust God and take a leap of faith. Faith in God requires action. Trust and LEAP!

V. Keep your eyes on God. LEAP, and don't allow your faith in God to waver.

VI. Trust the hand of God. Hold on to God's unchanging hand, and DON'T LET GO!

VII. Never doubt Him. Let nothing make you doubt Him; you know too much about Him.

As For Me and My House

"And if it seem evil unto you to serve the Lord, choose you this day whom ye will serve; whether the gods which your fathers served that were on the other side of the flood, or the gods of the Amorites, in whose land ye dwell: but as for me and my house, we will serve the Lord" (Joshua 24:15).

These were exciting times for the people of Israel. It was a time of hope, prosperity, and blessings. They had defeated their enemies and claimed the Promised Land. Each of the tribes had received their inheritance, and now they could settle down and enjoy life a little. Exciting as these times were, it was also a perilous time for the people! There was the danger that they would forget where they came from, how they had gotten to where they were, and what the Lord had done for them. There was the danger that they would begin to adopt the idolatrous religion of the Canaanites who still lived around them. There was the danger that they would fall into a state of complacency, a state in which they might feel that they could let their guard down just a little because of security and substance.

These were dangerous times for Israel indeed! In the midst of this situation, Joshua stands up to deliver to the people a challenge from the Lord. Joshua commands them to choose *whom they will serve*. Notice Joshua did not say *if* you will serve because we really are not left the option of not serving anyone. We will all serve someone - either the devil (intentionally or not) or the LORD. God wants them to dedicate themselves to Him and His work. He does not want them trying to live for Him on the one hand and the gods of Canaan on the other. The clear message of this passage is simple. God wants wholehearted dedication or nothing! Joshua was a wise man who looked at this situation sensibly, and he made the intelligent choice to say as for me and my house, we will serve the LORD. Joshua also understood that he, as the priest of his family, was charged with the responsibility to see that his whole house served the LORD. He had the job of representing his whole house before God. But as for me and my house indicates that Joshua's determination was based solely upon his relationship with God. Joshua did not consider the opinions of others, only his relationship with God and God alone. Joshua would serve God no matter what anyone else did. There was one God in his life, and that God was the LORD.

Men, it is our God-given right and responsibility to lead and care for our homes, and we must take this responsibility seriously. God commended Abraham because he commanded his household to keep the way of the Lord: *"For I know him, that he will command his children and his household after him, and they shall keep the way of the LORD, to do justice and judgment; that the LORD may bring upon Abraham that which he hath spoken of him"* (Genesis 18:19). This was no passive work accomplished by a spiritual weakling. If we as men desire to be respected by our wives, we must take charge of our homes and our children and command our households to follow in our footsteps. That means that we are the rule makers and the rule enforcers. The work of raising and teaching our children and guiding our households should never rest wholly upon the wife and mother. God has created our wives to be "helpmeets" or helpers to us. Therefore, it is our job and duty to lovingly, yet firmly, guide our homes.

As the Commander of his home, it is a man's responsibility to provide an authoritative order to his household that commands the family to *"keep the way of the Lord."* The Commander must determine tailor-made rules that align with his Joshua decision, "But as for me and my house, we will serve the LORD." I believe two primary areas are imperative in making a Joshua decision for your home:

I. Communication

Communication within the family is essential because it enables members to express their needs, wants, and concerns to each other. Open and honest communication creates an atmosphere that allows family members to express their differences as well as love and admiration for one another. It is through communication that family members can resolve the unavoidable problems that arise in all families.

Keeping a family together is not an easy task, and the task progressively becomes more difficult in a world where families are becoming more divided and falling apart every day. The responsibility of keeping your family together can be extremely stressful, and the Word of God proves that God's idea of family has been under attack since the beginning of time; it didn't just fall apart overnight. One of the greatest examples of family stress is found in Genesis 4:1-15, when Adam's family experienced stress and tension after their oldest son, Cain, killed his younger brother, Abel. If that's not family stress, I don't know what is. Yet, regardless of the situations, we face in life, God always has a plan. The stresses and storms of life have torn some families to shreds and made other families stronger. As the leader of the home, it is the man's responsibility to give an account for the members of his family. He needs to know his family's whereabouts at all times.

I am sure my Mama had no earthly idea that her every move was making such a significant impact on my life. Before I even had a family, I carried a vision of my family and friends seated around the dinner table after worship service. On Saturday's my Mama would send me to attend church at the Seventh Day Adventist Church while she went into town to take care of business. Before she left for town, she would always prepare a brown bag lunch for me to take. On this particular Saturday, I found a quiet spot to sit and enjoy the view while eating my lunch. About 20 yards away from me in a framed no door, no window building, I could see Elder Archie Thomas, the Pastor of the Seventh Day Adventist Church in Eldrick District, his family and another Pastor and his family gathered around the dinner table intensely listening to every word that came out of Elder Thomas's mouth. Although I wasn't seated right next to him, being outside gave me the best view ever. Watching them from a distance allowed me to see just how vital it is for a family to feast at the dinner table. I saw it, and I wanted it for the family that God would one day bless me to have. When the Lord blessed me with my own family, I made a Joshua decision and carried this tradition into my home, and to this day, my family shares Sunday dinner with us all seated at the dinner table.

It was important to me that I carried the tradition my Mama set for our family into my own family. Yvonne and I use our dinner table as the centerpiece of our home. In our home, our conservatory became my 'Boardroom,' and our family dinner table became my 'Command Centre.' From weeknight dinners to family celebrations, we gathered around our table not only to share food but to communicate with our children. In our 'Boardroom,' we would laugh together, pray together, plan together, and eat together. Our dinner table, our 'Command Centre,' became our place of community, a place that offered our family love, support, and a safe haven. This was one of my *"As For Me and My House"* decisions, and to date, it has been one of the best decisions I have made as a man, husband, and father.

Establishing my Boardroom gave my family one of the greatest gifts on earth, an open line of communication. One of the most difficult challenges facing families today is finding time to spend together. According to a recent Wall Street Journal survey, 40% of the respondents stated that lack of time was a more significant problem for them than the lack of money (Graham & Crossan, 1996). With our busy schedules, it isn't easy to find sufficient time to spend with one another in meaningful conversations. Families must make time to communicate, and family dinner time is a perfect time.

Gathering my family was actually the easy part. Learning how to communicate with them effectively, now that was a horse of a different colour. As the leader of my home, to effectively communicate with my family, I had to learn to be an active listener. An essential aspect of effective communication is listening to what others are saying. Being an active listener involves trying your best to understand the point of view of the other person. Whether listening to Yvonne or one of my children, I had to learn to pay close attention to their verbal and non-verbal messages. I had to acknowledge and respect their perspectives. When listening to your spouse or your children, simply nodding your head or saying, "I understand," conveys that you care about what he or she has to say. Another aspect of active listening is seeking clarification if you do not understand the other family member; this can be done by merely asking, "what did you mean when you said?" or "did I understand you correctly?"

Not all family members communicate in the same manner or at the same level. This is especially true when your children are young. When communicating with young children, it is important to listen carefully to what they are saying without making unwarranted assumptions. It is also important to take into consideration the ages of your children and the fact that all children do not mature at the same level. As the leader of your family, it would be beneficial to understand that communication with your spouse and communication with your children will not be the same. In addition to carefully listening to what is being said, we must learn to pay close attention to the non-verbal behaviours of other family members. For example, a spouse or child may say something verbally, but their facial expressions or body language may be telling you something completely different. In cases such as these, it is important to find out how the person is really feeling. For effective communication to happen in your family, it is the man's responsibility to take the time and identify the characteristics of each one of his family members.

Will all of the results be positive? Just as it was not for Adam's family, it may not be so for your family as well. Your job is to trust God, seek His face, and remain positive. Even in the midst of trouble, it is necessary to address problems between family members or deal with negative situations and keep all communication primarily positive. Marital and family researchers have discovered that unhappy family relationships are often the result of negative communication patterns, including constant criticism, contempt, and defensiveness. It is important for family members to compliment and encourage one another verbally.

Communication is a key to every man's *"As For Me and My House,"* Joshua decision. As the leader of your home, it is up to you to decide that your family will communicate in healthy ways that lead to effective problem-solving and provide the foundation for each of your family members to be more satisfied with their relationships as a family member.

II. Worship God Together -

Statistics show that over 60 percent of churchgoers in the average congregation is female. About 25 percent of married Christian women have husbands who will not attend church with them, which doesn't account for the vast majority of Christian families who have no prayer life or church life at all. These numbers are a disgrace to the honour of manhood. As the commanders of our homes, we must not only lead our families to the household of faith, but we must lead our families in prayer at home as well. If there's one earthly image that best signifies a healthy, spiritually grounded Christian family, it's that of a father on his knees in prayer. Our prayer life as fathers and husbands not only creates the foundation for our own lives but for the life of our family. Children need to see and hear their fathers worship God physically. Wives need to see it, too. The example it sets is invaluable, and the spiritual rewards are limitless.

Introducing our families to Christ is not to be taken lightly. As the leader of the family, it is the man's responsibility to ensure that his children learn to cherish their worship experience and not make attending church seem like a chore. Children can feel the difference between duty and delight. Therefore, the first and most important job of a parent is to fall in love with the worship of God. You can't impart what you don't possess. It is hard to overestimate the good influence of families doing valuable things together day in and day out, week in and week out, year in and year out. Worship is the most valuable thing a human can do to honour God.

Worshipping as a family provides parents unparalleled opportunities to teach their children the great truths of our faith. The message of Christ unfolds, and the music and lyrics become familiar. The message of the music starts to sink in, and the worship response comes naturally. The choir makes a lasting impression with a kind of music the children may hear at no other time. Even if most of the sermon goes over their heads, the worship experience allows the children to hear and remember remarkable things that will help to shape their future. As the leader of his home, a man must learn to question his children after the worship service and then explain things. Making this investment in your child's walk with God increases their desire to know more. As a result, the children's capacity to participate will begin to soar. Children who are taught to embrace the worship experience have positive and happy attitudes fostered by the parents. As leaders of our families, it is our responsibility to lay the foundation for our children and live in such a manner that the precious memories of our family worship provide our children with a portrait of their family focusing toward God. Our worship should be so authentic and valuable that it creates a thirst for God that is forever etched in their minds and in their hearts. This portrait should mirror Proverbs 22:6, *"Train up a child in the way he should go: and when he is old, he will not depart from it."* As a result, the seeds that we have sown and valuable lessons that we have taught to our children creates a nonverbal picture of family worship that grows richer and richer in the child's mind and heart as he matures in appreciation for his family and in awe at the greatness of God.

My *"As For Me And My House"* decision for my family to worship together enhanced two areas of my family's life, Commitment, and Compassion:

A. Commitment — The one principle God places first is commitment. The word means "to give in charge or trust, to deliver for safekeeping." A family's strength is defined by their level of commitment to God and each other. Commitment to God and commitment to others are related. If one is committed to God, he or she is more likely to be able to commit to another person and be responsible for that commitment. The commitment begins with spouses who have taken a solemn responsibility to love and care for each other and their children and honour marital vows with complete fidelity. Further, it warns that husbands and wives will one day be held accountable before God for the discharge of family obligations. National studies have shown parental commitment to marriage and family was associated with fewer behaviour problems in children and less conflict among parents and children.

B. Compassion — Compassion may be defined as sorrow for another's troubles, thus having an urge to help them. Christ was able to have compassion for us because, through the mystery of the Incarnation, He became one of us! *"For we have not an high priest which cannot be touched with the feeling of our infirmities; but was in all points tempted like as we are, yet without sin"* (Hebrews 4:15). He put himself in our place so he could see the world from our point of view. Through the miracle of the new birth, he helps us put ourselves in his place to see the world from His perspective. So compassion is the ability to imagine yourself in another person's place—to feel their pain, sense their need, have an urge to help them. When life seems challenging, the home should be where one can find love, compassion, and warmth. Every family member should feel reassured that someone understands and cares about how they feel. The compassion felt and experienced at home inspires us all to be more compassionate to others.

The decision for my family to worship together was never one up for debate. According to Ephesians 6:4, , it was my duty. It was how my

Mama raised me and the training that continued when I moved to the United Kingdom with my parents. Ministry was never a choice for my family; it is who we were. Ministry was my roots, and ministry is who I am; therefore, ministry is who my family became as well. As leaders of our families, every man must understand that it is his responsibility to teach his children about Christian values. Unfortunately, every day of your child's life will not be sunny; there will be happy days and sad days, ups and downs, high moments, and low moments; trouble will find their address. Instilling Christian values in their lives will help your child to be able to handle all of the things that life might throw their way. As we all know, life is full of changes, but the one thing we can be certain of is that our God remains the same and doesn't ever change.

Regardless of the circumstances, *"As For Me and My House, We Will Serve The Lord."*

CHAPTER IV

DISCIPLINE TRANSFORMED

MY MESSAGE

During the Lord's earthly ministry, he clothed the naked, fed the hungry, healed the sick, and raised the dead. He demonstrated gospel principles by action. After the resurrection of the Saviour, he gathered His Apostles on a mountain in Galilee and instructed them, saying: *"Go ye therefore, and teach all nations, baptizing them in the name of the Father, and of the Son, and of the Holy Ghost"* (Matthew 28:19). Here Christ delivered to his apostles the great charter of His kingdom in the world, which was to send them out as His ambassadors, and in doing so, He gives them their credentials. This command is one of the most vital commandments He has given—a divine, apostolic commission, and, in a general sense, it applies to all members of His church today. Notice the command is to *"**go and to teach**."* The ministry assignment is further explained in Matthew 28:20, *"Teaching them to observe all of the things whatsoever I have commanded you: and, lo, I am with you always, even to the end of this age. Amen."* This is a command to teach God's truth to man.

Acknowledge Your Ambassador Assignment

A disciplined lifestyle paved the way for my Ambassador Assignment. A calling that is emphasised in the writings of the Apostle Paul, *"How then shall they call on him in whom they have not believed? and how shall they believe in him of whom they have not heard? and how shall they hear without a preacher?"* (Romans 10:14). Indeed, being called to preach the Gospel of Jesus Christ is a fundamental emphasis of the Church, but it is equally important for that same Man of God to live the life he preaches about. A life that screams from the rooftops, *"the works that I do in my Father's name, they bear witness of me"* (John 10:25). A disciplined man never claims to be a perfect man for there is only one perfect man, and His name is Jesus Christ, Son of the Living God, but a disciplined man strives daily to be more like Him so that when others see him, they get a glimpse of the Father.

A disciplined man understands that his life is a significant part of his witness. If my relationship with Christ isn't vital, then I don't have a lot to share. People not only listen to your words, but they also look at your life. Does this mean that I am a perfect man? Again, no. Remember, there was only one perfect man. Even with our best attempts, we fail and aren't always a good example, so our only hope is to come to God and surrender to Him. It's nothing that we can do. It's God's work. My best advice to any man with a desire to please God and share his faith is to live a godly life. Non-Christians often look at Christians as hypocrites because we say one thing but do another. Show those close to you that you care— spend time with them, help to meet their needs, and offer to listen when they have problems. You may not be able to answer all of their questions, but they can't deny the testimony of what Christ has done in your life.

My Mama's prophetic words, ***"He is a disciplined boy,"*** shaped my life for service unto God. Whether it was driving the church bus, cleaning the church after service, encouraging and motivating others, or preaching the Gospel of Jesus Christ, it all came as second nature to me because I had been moulded and shaped for His service. However, when I was ordained as an Elder of the church, something sparked inside me.

The Elder's position meant that I was called to even greater responsibility and a visible role of leadership within the church. It was leadership service that warranted the position, but it wasn't until I accepted an Elder's title that I permitted myself to lead. The position of an Elder requires commitment, sacrifice, and integrity, and by taking the vow to serve, I made it my vow to give God my best service. To prepare for the work at hand, I enrolled in a Pastoral Course offered by the United Pentecostal Church entitled 'For Preachers Only.' It was an excellent course that prepared me for my role. Just as with any job, the ministry's work takes up a lot of time, so in turn, it deserves time vested in preparation and commitment.

Prepare to GO

Every responsible man must understand the vitality of preparation. The commandment to *"go and to teach"* requires a level of commitment that will shift your entire lifestyle. To fulfill the *"go and teach,"* commandment a leader must be ready at all times. There is no time to get ready; a leader must be ready! A leader must invest in the betterment of himself to ensure that he is well prepared to lead his family and God-given assignment. I believe mentorship is essential to the preparation of any leader. Mentoring is essential, not only because of the knowledge and skills one can learn from their mentor, but also because it provides an opportunity for on-the-job training and builds an accountability relationship. I am so grateful that I did not have to look far for someone to help mould and shape me as a leader in ministry; I had the awesome privilege of serving under my earthly father, Bishop Joshua Emmanuel Brooks. Although ministry was never my plan, it was definitely God's plan. Once I arrived in England, I immediately began working to support my father in his ministry endeavours. There were things that needed to be done to help advance his ministry, and without a thought, I jumped in to assist my father. The thought of becoming a preacher never once crossed my mind, but it was evident that my Mama's prophecy was always at work in my life. It may be safe to assume that my father took note of my disciplined lifestyle, and the Lord allowed my father to see me as a trusted leader. First, I became a Deacon under his leadership, then a Minister, then an Elder/Pastor, and I began pastoring one of his locations. My father pastored churches in Stafford, Wolverhampton, and Birmingham, and over time, he instructed me to go to the Birmingham location to help keep the church in order. Eventually, I became an Overseer. Little did I know the Lord was using him to prepare me for one of my *"go and to teach"* ministry assignments.

I treasure the blessing of growing up in Jamaica with my Mama, but I longed for a relationship with my father. Like most young men, I desired that father-son relationship. My Mama did an amazing job raising me, but there is nothing in the world that can replace a father-son relationship, and it did my heart all the good to work with him in ministry. In the spring of 1989, I went with my father to Boston, Massachusetts, to witness his consecration as a Bishop. Not only was this an amazing event to share with my father and my first time preaching in the United States, but this was also our first intimate trip as father-son. Up until this time, my father and I had never spent any alone time together. For the first time, it was just he and I. We shared a room, slept in the same bed, and had man-to-man conversations. This trip allowed us to develop the father-son relationship I had longed for.

The time spent with my father enhanced the "*go and to teach*" commandment on my life and, the time had come to put my faith into action. The congregation at the Birmingham location was small in number, a drastic change from the usual church setting that I had become accustomed to at the Stafford location. The Birmingham attendance had begun to decline for various reasons; transportation issues, some congregants moved away, and some even changed their membership to other churches. The Birmingham location had dwindled down to eight people, including children, attending the Sunday morning services. So many absences were left unaccounted for, and this was disheartening to me. I was assigned to go to the Birmingham location by my father, and what I thought was a temporary assignment became a permanent one. It was a struggle to pay the rent and keep petrol in both the car and the church van. Although I felt disappointed at the church's growth's stagnation, I believed that one day it would change. During this time in my life, the Lord began to increase my faith level as a man of God.

Without a doubt in my mind, I knew the Birmingham assignment was from God. There were times that I felt like my work was in vain, and I wanted to give up, but there was something on the inside that wouldn't allow me to walk away and give up; that something was my faith in God.

The Apostle Paul defines faith in Hebrews 11:1, *"Now faith is the substance of things hoped for, the evidence of things not seen."* Faith is trust, assurance, and confidence in God, and a disciplined man understands that his service and obedience show his living faith to God. Our faith is like a muscle; it can be strengthened, it can be weak, or it can be strong, depending on how much you use it. God will increase our faith if we fervently ask and draw close to Him. Once I understood this, I realised that my earthly father wasn't trusting me; he trusted my faith. It's like when the father, seeking help from Jesus for his son, said, *"Have pity on us and help us, if you possibly can"* (Mark 9:22 TEV). Jesus replied, *"What do you mean, 'If I can'? ... Anything is possible if a person believes"* (Mark 9:23 NLT). Just like the Lord had given a big assignment to Noah to build an ark, Abraham to be the father of a great nation, Joseph to be the leader to save his people, and Nehemiah to build the wall around Jerusalem, the Lord had given me a big assignment to lead the Birmingham congregation. The assignment required great faith that said, Lord, I Believe! The Bible tells us that God *"by his mighty power at work within us is able to do far more than we would ever dare to ask or even dream of — infinitely beyond our highest prayers, desires, thoughts, or hopes"* (Ephesians 3:20 LB). In other words, if a dream comes from God, it will be so big in your life that you can't do it on your own. If you could do it on your own, you wouldn't need faith. And if you don't have faith, you do not please God, because the Bible says whatever is not of faith is sin (Romans 14:23). A disciplined man understands that God will never tell you to do something that contradicts His truth. It is up to us to take a leap of faith and trust God to work within our lives to build our faith.

Faith Is Our Belief In Action

My faith in God saw me through the most challenging times. I believed that God had called me to the Birmingham location, and with faith, patience, and good works, the growth would come. I would put on my robe to encourage myself, and I would sing songs of encouragement in the church sanctuary. Matthew 7:7 encourages us to *"Keep on asking, and you will receive what you ask for. Keep on seeking, and you will find. Keep on knocking, and the door will be opened to you"*. I put my faith in God into action by speaking the lyrics, "Come on in the ark now, it's gonna rain" into existence. Singing these lyrics was my response to speak the things I desired into existence. The songs and prayers of my friends and family kept me going. Sunday after Sunday, my faith in God remained steadfast that God would keep his promises and deliver me from this dry place. I continued to pray, read, and believe the Word of God, I continued to sing encouraging hymns, and I held onto the encouragement my family showered me with. And just like God promised, I looked up one day, and the church started filling up. Anytime we demonstrate faith, we're relying on something or someone other than ourselves. When you sit in a chair, you're relying on the chair's manufacturer to produce something that will hold you up. When you step in a lift, you're relying on the lift to take you to the floor above or beneath you successfully. Faith in God means we rely on Him and depend on His reliability. Having faith means believing that God is bigger, greater, and better than me—and he loves me greatly. A disciplined man understands that God's ways are incomprehensible: *"For my thoughts are not your thoughts, neither are your ways my ways," saith the Lord. "For as the heavens are higher than the earth, so are my ways higher than your ways, and my thoughts than your thoughts"* (Isaiah 55:8–9). We are so precious to God that His highest thoughts are about us; they can't be counted (Psalm 139:17–18). In accepting that God's ways are far better than our own, we can release that which we cannot manipulate or guarantee—our future. Choosing to release control to the only One who is the Way, Truth, and Life gives us peace and security.

Often we equate faith with a mental assent to the facts when faith, however, is synonymous with action; apart from action, there is no faith. In fact, there isn't even a noun form of the word "faith" in Hebrew. Faith is only expressed as a verb because faith never exists apart from the action. The saints in Hebrews 11 became famous for something they didn't even have a name for because apart from action, faith does not exist. Noah *constructed* an ark, Abraham *left* his home, Jacob *blessed* his grandsons, Joseph *instructed* about his bones, Moses *chose* to be mistreated, Joshua *fought*. Each of these men had faith and were disciplined in understanding that faith is a conviction expressed in a choice. It starts with a belief, but if this "belief" does not lead to obedience, it is not yet faith. Your "belief" does not become true faith until you act upon it in obedience. I believe it is safe to say that faith is our belief in action. The Lord had been faithful to his promises, and the time had come for me to put my faith into action. Weekly my family and I were travelling back and forth from Stafford to Birmingham to attend church service, prayer service, and bible study. In 1999, I put my faith into action and moved my family from Stafford to Birmingham. For the ministry and the church to grow, church leadership needed to be present within the Birmingham community. I saw the move as an opportunity to make a difference in the lives of the people I pastored. Being so far away made it impossible to reach the people effectively. I genuinely believe that for a ministry to grow, its leadership must be visible amongst its community. The move allowed me to reach my community on a larger scale, which made a more significant difference and provided even more excellent opportunities to transform lives.

Order My Steps Lord

Taking the step to move my family to Birmingham once again required me to trust that God would order my steps. Again I had to put my faith into action and found comfort in the encouraging words of the text, *"The steps of a good man are ordered by the Lord: and he delighteth in his way"* (Psalm 37:23). The Lord promised that he would go ahead of me and clear the pathway for the life of my family. Every good man can find strength in knowing that when the Lord covers him, He is also protecting his family, and He promises to lead, guide, and direct our every step. In my heart, I knew that the move to Birmingham was the right move, but initially, the move with my family was nerve-racking. Although Stafford and Birmingham are only about thirty miles apart, the cities are very different, and my family was forced to adjust our lives to fulfill the ministry calling in Birmingham. The difficulty in finding a place for my family to reside didn't make matters any easier.

For two months, November 27, 1999, to January 26, 2000, my family was divided and lived in different locations. Yvonne and I were living with a couple from the church in one home while Rebecca resided with a different church member, and Adam and Matthew were living with another sister from the church. This set-up was nothing like what we were accustomed to in Stafford. As a man, this was hard to accept, but I pressed my way through it and made sure to see my children every day after school and Yvonne, and I kept them active in the church. I sincerely believed that taking this step of faith and moving to Birmingham aligned with God's will and provided an opportunity to grow the Lord's church. It was hard, but I kept the faith, and in the end, it paid off.

My faith cried, "Come on in the ark now, it's gonna rain," and the Lord answered my cry, and the congregation experienced continued growth. My faith in God led me to take action and walk away from my full-time secular job to make an even more substantial impact within our church community. Leaving my secular job for full-time ministry allowed me to sit on various boards and committees, speak at numerous events, and provide one-to-one counselling to countless members and couples. However, the move also meant a significant decrease in my salary. I lost two-thirds of my salary, and now I had to take care of my family on one-third of what we were accustomed to living on. Things were often tight and uncomfortable, but my faith was in God, and my mind was made up to preserve. In the midst of it all, I could see my faith at work. Our church grew through structural and cultural changes. Although I wanted to remain, the cultural differences presented conflict, which forced me out of the Mount Peniel Church of God in Christ Apostolic-UK. On 7 October 2000, New Jerusalem Apostolic Church was born out of the previous Mount Peniel Church. Growth under my leadership didn't stop there. In 2003, the church experienced another quantum leap as New Jerusalem officially became a part of the Jabula International Ministries under the previous Continental Bishop, Bishop Keith, and Pastor Winnie McLeod and Jabula founder, Bishop Tudor and Pastor ChiChi Bismark.

Faith Tried and Tested

We've all read or heard the story of Noah and the ark and how people laughed at and ridiculed him for building a gigantic boat in the middle of the desert. He listened to their insults for over one hundred years. But, he never gave up or turned his back on God. He was given a job to do, and he didn't quit until it was complete. He showed a tremendous amount of perseverance to do what he did. Perseverance is a fruit that every disciplined man must possess to be part of God's Kingdom. Perseverance is the ability to endure ill-treatment from life or at the hands of others without lashing out or paying back. As a young boy, I witnessed the NEVER Quit, NEVER Give-up spirit my Mama possessed. Any commitment she made, she maintained and completed her mission to the end. Her reactions to the blows life hit her with were similar to the ridicule Noah faced when building the ark and coincidentally similar to the challenges I began to encounter after walking away from my full-time job.

Perseverance is a command from God. The commandment is found in Revelations 3:7-10: *"To the angel of the church in Philadelphia write: These are the words of him who is holy and true, who holds the key of David. What he opens no one can shut, and what he shuts no one can open. I know your deeds. See, I have placed before you an open door that no one can shut. I know that you have little strength, yet you have kept my word and have not denied my name. I will make those who are of the synagogue of Satan, who claim to be Jews though they are not, but are liars—I will make them come and fall down at your feet and acknowledge that I have loved you. Since you have kept my command to endure patiently, I will also keep you from the hour of trial that is going to come on the whole world to test the inhabitants of the earth."* A person who has perseverance endures no matter what the trials or how much suffering or grief they have to go through. A disciplined man is willing to remain under trials, if necessary, and he will continue to follow God's way. By enduring such trials, he honours God and learns lessons the trials may teach.

The Apostle Paul comforts and encourages us in his writings found in the fifth chapter of the Epistle to the Romans 5:1-5: *"Therefore being justified by faith, we have peace with God through our Lord Jesus Christ: By whom also we have access by faith into this grace wherein we stand, and* rejoice in hope of the glory of God. And not only so, but we glory in tribulations also: knowing that tribulation worketh patience; And patience, experience; and experience, hope: And hope maketh not ashamed; because the love of God is shed abroad in our hearts by the Holy Ghost which is given unto us." A disciplined man can stand firm in his faith not because he is tough or strong, but because he knows that he has the Grace of God, the Spirit of God, and his hope is in the Kingdom of God. Unlike the famous cliche, 'when the going gets tough, the tough get going,' a disciplined man will hang in there and stand firm on the promises of God while going through physical struggles, financial struggles, or mental anguish. Perseverance is his willingness to stay strong and hang in there to see what the end will be. Any man that has the fruit of perseverance bears the right to testify "If it had not been for the Lord who was on my side." It is in the tough times, not the good times that we birth perseverance. Satan wants to know what it will take for us to give up. He is roaring about, trying to find out what it will take to shake us loose from the tree of life. What will shake us loose? Sickness? Losing our job? Financial problems? A disciplined man keeps his eyes on the cross, remains focused on the promises of God, and "hangs in there." He understands that the enemy will try any and everything to destroy him and his family, but he endures every trick of the enemy.

How does the disciplined man endure? He endures by relying on his faith in God. James, the half-brother of Jesus, shares words of encouragement in James 1:2-4: "Consider it pure joy, my brothers and sisters, whenever you face trials of many kinds, because you know that the testing of *your faith produces perseverance. Let perseverance finish its work so that you may be mature and complete, not lacking anything."* The circumstances that God allows to stretch our faith are called "trials": *"These trials will show that your faith is genuine. It is being tested as fire tests and purifies gold"* (1 Peter 1:7a NLT). I don't know about you, but failure is never an option in my life when faced with any test.

The testing of our faith develops perseverance, and it is the foundation upon which our perseverance is built. Perseverance and faith go hand in hand. When you continue to fall, but instead of giving up, you get right back up again, that's perseverance. A disciplined man does not quit. Instead, he keeps trying; he keeps knocking, and, finally, the door will open. Sometimes we fail in life physically or spiritually, but we must never give up. We have to stay in there for the long haul. We have to have faith, courage, tenacity, and stamina to keep going. Man of God, perseverance means more than endurance—more than merely holding on until the end. Here's the best illustration I can share to grasp your mind: Man of God, your life is in the hands of God like a bow and arrow in the hands of an archer. God is aiming at something you cannot see, but our Lord continues to stretch and strain, and every once in a while, you may think, "I can't take any more." God loves you so much that He pays no attention to your whines and whimpers; He continues to stretch you until His purpose for your life is in sight, and then and only then, He releases the arrow to fly. I encourage you to entrust your life into the hands of God.

Faith, by its very nature, must be tested and tried. And the real trial of faith is not that we find it difficult to trust God, but that God's character must be proven as trustworthy in our minds. Faith, as the Bible teaches it, is faith in God coming against everything that contradicts Him — a faith that says, "I will remain true to God's character whatever He may do." The highest and most significant expression of faith in the whole Bible is found in Job 13:15, *"Though He slay me, yet will I trust Him."* My faith and trust in God were tested, tried, and stretched when illness struck my body. I began to have unusual pain in my body that led me to see my General Practitioner. My symptoms led him to believe I showed signs of an irritable bladder or having an enlarged prostate which, was normal for a fifty-year-old black man, so nothing was done to help my situation. As time went on, my symptoms became worse, and eventually, my doctor asked me to come to the hospital for a biopsy to be performed. The biopsy results began the testing and trying of my faith; I was diagnosed with prostate cancer. There is never a good time for illness to come into your life, and this definitely was not a good time for me. The church was growing, the ministry was demanding, and I was enrolled in Bible School in Scotland. I was not at my strongest physically, but I never allowed my illness to prevent me from carrying out my ministry role. Despite the pain, I continued with my studies. In April 2006, I became extremely ill whilst in Scotland and had to return to Heartlands Hospital in Birmingham immediately. Again, nothing was done to help me. The doctor gave me stronger tablets and encouraged me to get more rest. This continued until the 6th of May, when the doctors discovered that my pain was caused by water retention, eight pints of 'dead water' to be exact. This water had been causing me immense pain for nearly three weeks, and it could have poisoned me and quickly killed me. Although I was diagnosed with cancer, I had no fear. The doctors then consulted Yvonne and me, and we decided to move forward with surgery and scheduled it for 2 PM on Thursday, 13th of July 2006. My faith and trust were in God, and I had total confidence that everything would be alright with God on my side. I was so confident that I found myself ministering to a Muslim staff nurse while they were prepping me for surgery without even thinking about it. I was lying on my back in the theatre, and a Muslim staff nurse began to share her marital problems with me. I could have failed my test and very well brushed her off or selfishly ignored her, but this woman was hurting and in need of spiritual counsel. I couldn't walk away from an opportunity to be used by God and turn around and expect him to bless me. Instead, I put myself aside and gave her appropriate counsel. Again I was faithful to God, and the Lord blessed my faithfulness.

Routinely my surgery should have taken two and a half hours, but instead, it took six, almost seven hours. The doctors ran into serious complications. It wasn't until they opened me up that they discovered that my prostate had intertwined with my bladder. It was the largest they had ever encountered, and the process of removing it was complicated, BUT GOD! Dr. Tate, one of my doctors who is also a Christian, said, "Mr. Brooks, sometimes God saves people by miracles, and sometimes he uses doctors. In your case, on Thursday night, we thought we lost you."

And to think if I would not have continued to push and push my doctors for the right answers, I may not be here today. A disciplined man does not quit. Instead, he keeps trying; he keeps knocking, and, finally, the door opens. Sometimes we fail in life physically or spiritually, but we must never give up. We have to stay in there for the long haul. We have to have faith, courage, tenacity, and stamina to keep going.

The power to persevere is essential to your life. Despite how your situation may look, you cannot give up. You must keep your eyes on the cross and know that our God rewards our faithfulness. There is one mind-blowing thing you must keep in mind when you work for the Lord; remember, what you do for the Lord is never in vain. When you put your faith into action and work for the Lord, you can trust that your labour, sweat, tears, tenacity, faith, courage, and stamina are never in vain. You never have to worry about the ones that laughed at you or those who did not believe in you. Your rewards do not come from them. They laughed at Noah, but when the floodwaters began to rise, I am sure many of his naysayers wished they would have helped him build the ark. The Apostle Paul reminds us, *"Therefore, my beloved brethren, be steadfast, unmovable, always abounding in the work of the Lord, forasmuch as ye know that your labour is not in vain in the Lord"* (I Corinthians 15:58). The word vain, translated in Greek, means 'without gift.' Our God recognises our hard work and our labour, and regardless if others think you deserve it or not because you remained faithful even when the odds were stacked against you, you will not go without receiving a gift for your perseverance. Somehow, I was able to take care of my family on one-third of my salary, maintain the church's rent, keep petrol in the church van to transport members, withstand the massive decline in church membership, and fight cancer. Yet, my faith in God persevered, and my labour was not in vain. The church grew, the Lord healed my body of cancer, and I was elevated to the Bishopric. Again, the prophecy my Mama spoke over my life came to fruition. Her prophetic words, *"He is a disciplined boy,"* overflowed my life, and I became Bishop Melvin Alphonso Brooks. My faith in God was tried and tested, but through it all, I persevered, and the Lord blessed me beyond my wildest imagination.

Unshakeable Faith

Faith is not some weak and pitiful emotion. Faith is strong and vigorous confidence built on the fact that God is holy love. And even though you cannot see Him right now and cannot understand what He is doing, you know Him. Faith is the supreme effort of your life—throwing yourself with abandon and total confidence in God. Here's the truth, no matter who you are, how saved you may be, how dedicated you are to working in ministry, it doesn't matter how many bible verses you have memorised or if you are at the church every time the church doors are open, trouble will find your address. James taught about faith, telling us that true faith is demonstrated by what we are, how we live, and what we do. Let's take a closer look at the book of James. James, the author of James's epistle, identifies himself by name but describes himself as *"a servant of God and of the Lord Jesus Christ"* (James 1:1). His letter deals more with Christian ethics than Christian theology. Its theme is the outworking of faith—the external evidence of internal conversion. A study of James' life provides some crucial lessons for us. His conversion gives testimony to the overwhelming power that came from being a witness of Jesus' resurrection: James turned from being a skeptic to a leader in the church based on his meeting the resurrected Christ. Unlike James, I did not witness Jesus' resurrection, but I can testify that it was Jesus that healed my body when cancer tried to overtake me. My witness echoes the lyrics of gospel artist Kurt Carr's song entitled, *I've Seen Him Do It.* Regardless of the circumstances life presents, I can stand firm in my faith in God because my testimony reminds me that the last time I was faced with trouble, God came through for me. A disciplined man understands that although he has faith in God, his faith can be grown and strengthened through life's hard times. The first chapter of James opens with a greeting and encouragement to remain joyful in the midst of trials because the outcome of this type of testing is perseverance and a faith that is mature and complete. James encourages that God is faithful to this process and will grant wisdom so we can endure it. James encourages us to ask God for the things we desire in life but to ask with a faith that is confident and not unwavering, *"But let him ask in faith, nothing wavering. For he that wavereth is like a wave of the sea driven with the wind and tossed"* (James 1:6). A faith that is confident in God because I have seen him do it!

A disciplined man is required to live the life that he preaches about with the understanding that believers are in a life-and-death battle for your faith. The enemy is determined to destroy the faith of all of God's elect, and the stronger your faith, the greater his attack will be on you and your family. When the enemy attacked my health, I stood firm in my faith and trusted God to heal my body. Because of God's grace, I walked away with victory over cancer. How many of you know the enemy didn't let up? Not at all. The enemy began to attack my daughter Rebecca and her husband, Patrick. Patrick and Rebecca, a vibrant young couple who are on fire for the Lord, desired to conceive a child. For nearly eight years, I watched this young couple experience a roller coaster of emotions, disappointments, stress, anger, and disbelief. As their father/Pastor, I shared words of comfort over the gravesites of my precious grandchildren. Losing a child is a painful experience for any parent. Rebecca was hurting, and as her father, I wanted to take that pain away. She and her unborn babies had shared heartbeats, a sound that she will never forget. Rebecca once said, "My child may not be here, but my child knows what my heartbeat sounds like from the inside." Although she did not have a child to hold in her arms, she will always carry those children in her heart. To witness my daughter and her husband struggle with child-birth was heartbreaking, but their amazing faithfulness and commitment to Christ made me trust God all the more. Rebecca's faith is strong, and she and Patrick never stopped believing God. She knew that her womb was blessed, and God would give her a child. The enemy tried to get my faith to waver, but little did he know I possessed an unshakeable faith. Patrick and Rebecca served faithfully in ministry and were devout to God, but they had to sit back and congratulate others on successful pregnancies and healthy births. This seemed unjust to the natural eye, but my faith in God reminded me that our God is a just God. Instead of becoming upset, angry, or doubting God, I continued to pray and stand firm in my faith. My faith said God can, and God will because I've seen Him do it! Instead of questioning God, my faith believed that in His timing, He would give them the desires of their hearts. I covered my family in prayer, knowing that their reward would eventually come, and God did it! The Lord kept his promise, and born to share my birth date was our first granddaughter, Jade Zara Lee Linton.

James says that instead of complaining, giving up, or giving in, take the hardships of life and use them to strengthen yourself. Here are ten things the Epistle James 1:2-8 teaches a disciplined man about trials:

1. We are to welcome trials with joy.

2. There will be various kinds of trials for us to rejoice in.

3. Trials test our faith.

4. Trials that test our faith produce steadfastness in our faith and our lives.

5. Trials produce faith and a life that lacks nothing.

6. Trials provide us an opportunity to trust God.

7. Trials provide us an opportunity for God to provide.

8. Trials provide us an opportunity to prove that we have faith and we do not doubt God.

9. Trials provide a test by which our faith can be measured.

10. God promises his blessings to those who remain steadfast under a trial.

A disciplined man is like the Apostle Peter when a ferocious attack came against his faith. His trust in Jesus put Satan in such an uproar that Satan asked permission to sift him to see if he would stand. *"Simon, Simon, behold, Satan hath desired to have you, that he may sift you as wheat: I have prayed for thee, that thy faith fail not: and when thou art converted, strengthen thy brethren"* (Luke 22:31-32). Satan desired to catch Peter in his rough state and separate Him from the Lord. In the midst of his adversity, the Lord offers Peter comforting words. *"I have prayed for thee, that thy faith fail not."* It is vital to take note of what Jesus did not pray for:

a. He did not pray that Satan would not put him through the sieve.

b. He did not pray, asking the Lord to let him have the easy road, no hard testings or trials.

c. He did not pray, asking the Lord to keep him from all suffering and pain.

However, the interesting fact lies within what Peter later wrote, *"Beloved, think it not strange concerning the fiery trial which is to try you, as though some strange thing happened unto you: But rejoice, inasmuch as ye are partakers of Christ's sufferings; that, when his glory shall be revealed, ye may be glad also with exceeding joy. If ye be reproached for the name of Christ, happy are ye; for the spirit of glory and of God resteth upon you: on their part he is evil spoken of, but on your part he is glorified".*

Peter had come to learn the value of being tested. It is as though the Lord is saying to Peter, Satan knows your broken parts, and he desires to take advantage of that to separate you from Me. I also know your damaged pieces and the weakness of your flesh, I know that before the sun rises tomorrow morning, you will have slept when you should have been praying, you will be drawing and using your sword at an inappropriate time, and you will have denied Me three times. Satan is going to take you through the sieve, but I am praying for you. What must it be like to hear the Lord saying, "I have been praying for you." Wouldn't you love to hear Jesus say, "I have been praying for you"? The beautiful and glorious truth of the matter is that He has and is praying for you always. Jesus prayed for Peter that his faith would not fail him. He knew that Peter would deny Him. He knew that in the hour of failure, Satan likes to move in with great force to condemn us. He is always using our failures as a wedge to drive us away from the Lord. Every time you sin, you can be sure he is going to move in on you, condemning you and asking, "How can you ever expect God to do anything for you when you have failed Him so many times." He loves to move in with discouragement and say, "You may as well give up; you are never going to make it. Look how hard you have tried, and you still sin miserably. God wants nothing to do with you; he has given up on you." Jesus knew the great test that Peter would be facing and how he would fail that test, thus coming under massive attack from the enemy, as Satan would seek to sift him like wheat.

Peter's strongest natural trait, courage, failed him. Remember, he was ready to step out onto the stormy sea at the bidding of Jesus but lacked the courage to put his faith into action. This is the same Peter that was ready to take on the whole band of soldiers who came to arrest Jesus. Peter was naturally a very courageous man. Interestingly, Satan often attacks us in the place of our greatest natural strength, and that is where he usually defeats us. We are often defeated in the area of our greatest natural strength, for we often have confidence in our ability and do not feel the need to rely on the Lord in those places. We are thus prone to have confidence in the strength of our flesh. Peter's courage may have failed him, but his faith did not fail him. Like Peter, we too may fail when sifted by Satan, but with the Lord praying for us, we always come up stronger as a result of the testing. That is one of the purposes that He has in allowing Satan to sift us, that we might discover that even in our places of greatest strength, we need to rely on Him and are thus much stronger in the end.

CHAPTER V
DISCIPLINE TRANSFORMED
MY MINISTRY

A journey of faith requires extraordinary discipline, a discipline with a strong commitment and dedication to God. There are three essential disciplines I want us to consider. First, Discipline of the Heart, which is our inner being; secondly, Discipline of the Word, the Bible; and, thirdly, Discipline of Service. These spiritual disciplines call for discernment, accountability, and direction to overcome our resistance and deafness about God's will for us.

Three Essential Areas of Discipline

Discipline of the Heart

Discipline of the Heart is perhaps the crucial spiritual discipline. Think about it; prayer is one of the most important things a Christian can do. This is when we communicate with God, and our prayer time should be taken very seriously. While there is significant theological meaning in prayer, it doesn't have to be complicated and difficult. It's something anyone can do anywhere at any time. Prayer is an opportunity to spend time with God. To understand the heart of God, you need to pray. Prayer is our tool to win the many battles of the enemy. Prayer gives us the strength and the faith to finish the race victoriously. Prayer changes us. When we spend time with God, he is working to change our hearts to be more like His. The more time we spend with Him, the more we are like Him. Our habits and lifestyles change. We no longer live a self-centred life but live a life focusing on others with a pure and sincere heart. Prayer changes us inside out.

Discipline of the Word

Discipline of the Word accompanied by both meditation and contemplative prayer is the way by which God's Word ultimately becomes woven into the very fabric of our being. Discipline of the Word then leads us to obedience. Over time it transforms our identity, our actions, and our walk of faith. Discipline of the Word includes hearing the Word of God, reading the Word of God, studying the Word of God, memorizing the Word of God, meditating on the Word of God, and obeying the Word of God. A disciplined man understands the importance of feeding on the Word of God. As Jesus said, *"Man shall not live by bread alone, but by every word that comes from the mouth of God"* (Matthew 4:4). It is through the regular, personal intake of the Bible that we come to know God better, understand His will for our lives, and experience God's transforming presence.

Discipline of Service

Discipline of Service is our commitment to serving others as Jesus called and exemplified. Our service is not about salvation; it is about our response to God. Serving God is not a choice; it is our duty. When we serve God, we allow our love for the Lord to flow in us from Him and then to others around us. Service builds and prepares us. Service builds strength in our character as we fulfill our responsibility for His Kingdom. Service also nurtures and strengthens us as a means of grace; as we grow, we serve. The more we serve, the more Christ-like we become. This is about using the best of what God has given to us, being obedient to Him, and serving Him. We are all called to serve, not as just pastors or Christian professionals, but as our relationship with Christ is woven into all, we do in life. This is our call to servanthood. In unison, these disciplines lead us to become free and obedient servants of the Lord. They allow us to become persons who hear God's voice even when calling us in faith to an unknown or uncomfortable place.

Called To Serve

The Lord called me to an unknown place to serve his people while attending a Fun Day at John Wheeldon Academy, Adam and Matthew's school. Spending quality time with my children was a top priority in my life, and attending Fun Day always brought so much joy to our lives. There I was, just leisurely lying in the grass, when one of the boy's friends, Richard Giles, just crawled across me and began playing with me. While the boys and I played in the grass, Richard's mother watched from afar. I had never met her before, but my encounter with her son led her to walk over to me to tell me that my caring nature made her believe that I would do well working in a prison. During more conversation, she informed me that a position for a Black Minority Ethnic (BME) Member on the Local Review of the Nationale Parole Board was available, and she identified me as a suitable candidate. In turn, she submitted my name as a candidate, and the results marked the beginning of my service as a chaplain in the prison system.

I served on the National Parole Board for three years and progressed to serving on the Board of Visitors (BOV). The prisoner's welfare became my main goal, and I worked to ensure that the prison upheld the government's laws. I won the respect of my peers and was asked to speak at the prison chapel to commemorate the release of Nelson Mandela from prison, which was indeed an honor. As a result of my speech, I became even more involved as a prison chaplain, but it wasn't long before the Chairperson of the board saw my dual roles as an obstacle. The Chairperson felt that serving on the board and serving as a chaplain presented a conflict of interest and instructed me to choose between the two. Forced to decide, I easily chose to continue serving as a chaplain because it was more rewarding and fulfilling. I received backlash from several of the board members because they did not want me to resign from the board, but I proudly stood by my decision because I knew in my heart that I was a preacher first and serving the people of God was my calling.

Little did I know that my decision to remain as a chaplain would lead me to serve as a lead chaplain one day. The lead chaplain of Drake Hall's Prison left his position to go to war. During a conversation on one Tuesday, I casually and jokingly said to the governor that perhaps I should be considered for the prison's lead chaplain. By regular requirements, I did not qualify for the position because, in those days, to be considered, you had to be a member of an Anglican Church. But God had other plans. By Friday of that same week, I became the Lead

Chaplain of Drake Hall's Prison. The prisoners and officers made the job challenging, but I persevered. I later advanced to become a prison keyholder. The position of keyholder was a very critical role that demanded a high level of trust and reliability. The work at Drake's Hall required additional responsibility outside of my ministry work but in the end; it was essential in building me as a Pastor and leader within my community. Serving others was a chief characteristic I learned as a young boy while tending to their ganja plants or climbing the trees to gather their fruit. Servanthood was embedded within my roots, and I carried this principle into my adult life.

Serving God should not be looked upon as a burden or a chore we must do. It is a response of our love and gratitude to the one we serve, and our response to service must come out of complete humility. It is our Fruit and character in action. The discipline of serving God is not something we are to do occasionally or when it is convenient. When there is an opportunity, we jump in, and as a faithful servant of God, we should always be open to opportunities regularly. The Lord has always provided me with numerous opportunities to serve him in great capacities. When I think back to my days of youth, I can quickly identify the four influential figures in my life, yet other than my Mama, I did not have anyone to help and guide me. True, my Mama did an AMAZING job raising me alone, but her resources were limited; she could only teach me what she knew. And for that reason, I desired to make a difference in the lives of young people. Young people are a valuable asset in our hands, but they need our help and our guidance. It is important that I help young people realise how to embody God's will for their lives. I must invest in my community by encouraging, inspiring, and motivating young people working to advance their education level. It has been my privilege to serve as a Chaplain on the Trustee Board of Wolverhampton University for over 20 years. As a Pastor and leader of God's people, I have a responsibility to be a voice within the community in which my sheep reside. I continue to maintain my community voice through organised chaplaincy in prisons, providing service at elderly homes, working with young people through the 'Transformation Centre,' an organised Food Bank that works with the local council to provide services to bring hope to the disadvantaged.

I can not take any credit for any of my achievements in life because if I stood on my strength alone, I would fall flat on my face. I owe it all to God. I pushed through every obstacle that life used to try and trip me up, yet somehow, I persevered and gained strength along the way. Without the support of my family, I would never have made it. The Lord blessed me with a woman of God designed just for me, and because of the love of Yvonne, my Proverbs 31 woman, I am a better man. My wife and children are my strength, and together, the Lord blessed us to accomplished so much. Ministry is not a job; it is a lifestyle. Ministry is the servant of God working to assure that every man, woman, and child receives the gift of John 3:16: *"For God so loved the world, that he gave his only begotten Son, that whosoever believeth in him should not perish, but have everlasting life."* There are many Sunday mornings that I sit on the pulpit and bask in the glory of God to see my family serving God faithfully in ministry. To witness my wife Yvonne laboring to encourage the women of God to be Women of

Purpose, my daughter Rebecca leading worship, my son Adam on the keyboard, and Matthew on the drums, I can't help but fall to my knees, throw my hands up and tell God thank you. My family has walked this ministry journey with me, and I am so grateful! I am honored and humbled to serve as the Senior Pastor of New Jerusalem Apostolic Church, the first appointed Presiding Prelate of Jabula New Life Ministries in Europe and Asia, and the Chief Operating Officer of Jabula New Life Ministries International.

As I look back over my life, I can reflect on words spoken by American author Ray Bradbury. In his novel Fahrenheit 451, Bradbury encourages the reader to leave something behind when he dies. He suggests leaving a child or a book or a painting or a house or a wall built or a pair of shoes made. Or a garden planted. Something your hand touched so when you die, and when people look at that tree or that flower you planted, they remember you. Bradbury says it doesn't matter what you do, as long as you change something from the way it was before you touched it into something that's like you after you take your hands away. He said the difference between the man who cuts lawns and a real gardener is in the touching. The lawn-cutter might just as well not have been there at all; the gardener will be there a lifetime." The first time I read this quote, I immediately got chills. Bradbury's words are not written in any one of the Bible's sixty-six books. Yet, his words echo the promises, instructions, and commandments pertinent to a man leaving behind his legacy.

Deuteronomy 6:5-9, *"You shall love the Lord your God with all your heart and with all your soul and with all your might. And these words that I command you today shall be on your heart. You shall teach them diligently to your children, and shall talk of them when you sit in your house, and when you walk by the way, and when you lie down, and when you rise. You shall bind them as a sign on your hand, and they shall be as frontlets between your eyes. You shall write them on the doorposts of your house and on your gates."*

Deuteronomy 12:28, *"Be careful to obey all these words that I command you, that it may go well with you and with your children after you forever, when you do what is good and right in the sight of the Lord your God."*

Proverbs 13:22, *"A good man leaves an inheritance to his children's children, but the sinner's wealth is laid up for the righteous."*

Proverbs 17:6, *"Grandchildren are the crown of the aged, and the glory of children is their fathers."*

Proverbs 22:6, *"Train up a child in the way he should go; even when he is old he will not depart from it."*

Leave A Legacy Behind

Every man has a responsibility to utilize his God-given gifts and talents to create a legacy that will impact lives far beyond his existence. Legacies are not created overnight, but with prayer and hard work, every man can responsibly generate a legacy that will take the next generation to a level we could only imagine. I genuinely believe that by grasping hold of the promises of Proverbs 13:22, a man develops a foundation for his life that is both good and honorable. When we strive to leave a legacy, we act with a selflessness that can only be beneficial for our family. Yes, I suppose someone could work hard to earn money so that a building is named after them when they die, but that is not the kind of legacy I am talking about. I am referring to creating a legacy that makes life better for those who come after us, not about building personal fame or recognition, but about helping others. After all, we won't be around to watch our legacy. To establish that which will last beyond us is selfless, and living with that in mind breaks the power of selfishness that tries so desperately to engrain itself in our lives.

I began this publication with my earliest recollection of my life at the tender age of 3. That is the earliest that I can recall that I, Melvin Alphonso Brooks, existed. I existed. It's In His word, He declares, *"The thief cometh not, but for to steal, and to kill, and to destroy: I have come that they might have life, and that they might have it more abundantly"* (John 10:10 KJV). The God we serve desires that we have an abundant life. The Greek translation of the word abundant means to exceed some number or measure or rank or need. The most significant distinction between living and existing comes from how much control you have over life decisions. A man who only exists feels as if everything is outside of his control, while the man who decides to live his life to the full lives knowing that he has the power to determine which path his life will take.

The decision to live for God is not a decision that can be made straddling the fence. Steve Jobs, the world-renowned co-founder of Apple, Inc., did something that could provide some guidance to us all. He would wake up each morning, look at himself in the mirror, and ask himself the same question, "If I was to die today, would I do what I am about to do?" If his answer were no too many days in a row, he would make a change. I think this is a good starting point for figuring out if you're living or just existing. If you're not getting excited or happy most days with what you're going to do, you need to take action and change something. Take inventory of every area of your life to ensure that you are living and not just existing. Steve Jobs' attitude is how I would describe someone who is living. He's not content with doing a routine simply because he did it the day before. He knows that you continually have to find something that is meaningful to you and makes you happy. Otherwise, you stop getting up in the morning because you want to, and you start getting up because it's obligatory. Every responsible, disciplined man has an obligation to be the best man that he can be for his family.

Transforming from a boy into a man is a process that requires discipline. My Mama spoke the words *"He is a disciplined boy,"* and her words not only defined my character, but her words were words of prophecy over my life. The transformation a boy endures into manhood requires him to possess a discipline that perseveres in living his life as a mirror image of his heavenly father. Therefore, a disciplined boy can never merely exist; he is commanded to live his life to the full, according to Romans 14:8, *"If we live, we live for the Lord; and if we die, we die for the*

Lord. So, whether we live or die, we belong to the Lord." A life well-lived is a life that is lived for the glory of God. We glorify God by having a Disciplined Heart, being Disciplined in the Word of God, and being a Disciplined Servant. This faith-filled journey is not easy, but if you place your trust in God, knowing that you will fulfill the obligation you have as a responsible man with God on your side. Live by the Fruit of the Spirit, make *"as for me and my house"* decisions, make every God ordered step in faith, reach back and pull the left behind during every *"go and to teach"* moment God provides you, and you too will leave a legacy behind that says, *"He is a disciplined boy."* Because I persevered, much like Steve Jobs, I, Melvin Alphonso Brooks, can look into the mirror and humbly say Lord, thank you! Thank you for moulding me into the **MAN** I have become, for manifesting the **MESSAGE** you have given me, and for blessing the **MINISTRY** you have entrusted into my hands!

MELVIN ALPHONSO BROOKS

'He is a disciplined boy transformed into a disciplined man.'

Transforming Lives. Forever.

Printed in Great Britain
by Amazon

55967840R00078